GETTING FROM HERE TO THERE

RELATIONAL PERSPECTIVES BOOK SERIES

Volume 32

RELATIONAL PERSPECTIVES BOOK SERIES

LEWIS ARON AND ADRIENNE HARRIS
Series Editors

GETTING FROM HERE TO THERE
Analytic Love, Analytic Process

Sheldon Bach

THE ANALYTIC PRESS

2006   Hillsdale, NJ   London

Published by
The Analytic Press, Inc., Publishers
    Editorial Offices:
    101 West Street
    Hillsdale, NJ 07642
    www.analyticpress.com

Designed and typeset (Latin 11/13) by
Christopher Jaworski, qualitext@verizon.net
Index by Cynthia Swanson

Chapter 1 was first published in © The Psychoanalytic Quarterly, 2001, *The Psychoanalytic Quarterly,* Vol. 70, No. 4, pp. 739–756. All rights and permissions granted. Chapter 3 was first published as "On Treating the Difficult Patient" in *The Modern Freudians,* edited by Carolyn S. Ellman and Stanley Grand, pp. 185–195, © 2000 by Jason Aronson, Inc. All rights and permissions granted. Chapter 4 appeared as "A Mind of One's Own" in *Symbolization and De-Symbolization,* edited by Richard Lasky, pp. 387–406, © 2002, Other Press. All rights and permissions granted. Chapter 7 is reprinted from *The Journal of Clinical Psychoanalysis,* Vol. 11, No. 2, pp. 225–255, by permission of International Universities Press, Inc., © 2002 by International Universities Press, Inc.

Library of Congress Cataloging-in-Publication Data

Bach, Sheldon
    Getting from here to there : analytic love, analytic process / Sheldon Bach
      p. ; cm. – (Relational perspectives book series ; v. 32)
    Includes bibliographical references and index.
    ISBN 0–88163–439–5
    1. Mind and body therapies. 2. Countertransference (Psychology).
    3. Psychoanalysis. 4. Love. I. Title. II. Series.
    [DNLM: 1. Professional–Patient Relations. 2. Countertransference
    (Psychology). 3. Love. 4. Psychoanalytic Therapy. 5. Transference
    (Psychology) WM 62 B118g 2005]
    RC489.M53B33   2005
    616.89'14—dc22

                                   2005057053

Printed in the United States of America
10 9 8 7 6 5 4 3 2 1

For Phyllis

CONTENTS

ACKNOWLEDGMENTS

My primary debt is to my patients and supervisees who must remain anonymous but who have literally taught me everything I know; some of them have generously given permission to use thoroughly disguised examples from our work together.

Many of the ideas in this book have been developed and discussed in my peer group of friends: Steven Ellman, Mark Grunes, Norbert Freedman, Irving Steingart, and, at one time, Martin Nass. This group has been meeting continually now for almost 40 years, and the collaboration and interpenetration has been such that it is sometimes impossible to know who first thought of any particular idea. I am extraordinarily grateful to them for their generosity and unwavering support and for both spiritual and vinous sustenance over the years.

I am very lucky to have so many dear friends and colleagues who have supported me in both good times and bad over the years I was writing this book. So I would like to thank for their care and support Graciela Abelin-Sass, Abbie Adams and Mark Silvan, Delia Battin and Eugene Mahon, Carolyn and Steve Ellman, Joyce and Norbert Freedman, Madelon Sann and Jerry Grobman, Mark Grunes, Arlene and Arnie Richards, Lynne and Robert Rubin, Susan and Steve Schulson, Mara and the sorely missed Lester Schwartz, Katherine and Kenneth Snelson, Joyce and Irving Steingart, Annie and Warren Weisberg, Jennie Weisberg and Mark Landsman, Allan Waltzman, and many others whom I cannot mention.

I would also like to thank my editors, Lew Aron and Adrienne Harris, whose comments and feedback were enormously helpful in preparing the book for publication.

Finally, I would like to thank my family, who have borne with me over these many years: my daughter, Rebecca, Renaissance scholar and proud mother of our darling granddaughter, Julia; dear Brendan and his family, Ellen and Keith; Eric and Judy; and, of course, Sonja and Verushka. I owe a special debt of gratitude to my son Matthew, who has scrupulously edited the entire book with a loving care that has made it far more coherent and reasonable than it otherwise would have been. Above all else, my debt is to my wife, Phyllis, without whose support and love nothing would have been possible for me.

PREFACE

The integration and disintegration of mind and body has fascinated me ever since I began to study psychology half a century ago.
Even as a child I was curious about how it was that some people
seemed at home in their bodies while others seemed to inhabit
them with ill grace, as if their bodies were temporarily on loan. As a
young man I witnessed the devastation of minds and bodies and
bodies politic in Europe during World War II.

After the war I lived in Europe for a number of years. When I
returned to America to begin my doctoral studies in psychology, I
happened by good luck to stumble into the Research Center for
Mental Health at New York University, where Klein, Holt, Rapaport, and others were conducting cutting-edge research into psychoanalytic theory.

I was excited and fascinated by the ongoing studies of alternate
states of consciousness: of dream imagery, of LSD trances, of subliminal stimulation. I was intrigued too by our ill-fated attempt to
increase the sale of peanuts at movies by subliminally projecting
EAT PEANUTS! onto the screen.

The atmosphere in which we all thrived was that of an academic, grant-supported, and research-oriented think-tank with a slightly nutty character, exemplified in my mind by a distinguished-looking Middle European psychiatrist who used to come to his laboratory cubicle on occasional afternoons, unpack an ancient violin, and play selected arias to experimental subjects while releasing vials of perfume in pursuit of his investigations into sensory synesthesia.

My own sense of unintegration and my interest in altered states and transformations that began in my childhood was compounded by my disruptive experiences as a GI: the sudden confrontation with life and death and the abrupt immersion in the strange and unfamiliar culture of a war-torn Europe.

I remember the culture shock that I experienced after the war when I was going to school at the Sorbonne on the GI Bill. In the United States, I had been given a taste of English literature from *Beowulf* to Thomas Wolfe in one crowded semester. In Paris the professor wrote on the blackboard one line of poetry, which, examined from many aspects, was going to be our text for the year. As an impressionable young man, I was smitten with what I saw as the European way of doing things, and it took me a long time to integrate these disparate perspectives.

But the existence of multiple perspectives became a given in my life, and it was fueled by the postwar thinkers, political scientists, and poets who were all, in their own ways, trying to see if any sense could be made of the great psychological traumas of the war and the Holocaust. Thus I became interested not only in Freud at a time in the 1950s when his presence dominated American psychiatry, but also in the great analytic traumatologists, such as Ferenczi and Winnicott, who seemed to me to be dealing with the very issues that I found so pressing.

Shortly after I arrived at New York University I was lucky enough to do some work on subliminal stimulation with George Klein that we published in 1958. This work set the stage for my doctoral thesis, which was an effort to investigate the effects of subliminal visual stimuli and altered states of consciousness. After graduation in 1960 I immediately began psychoanalytic training and shortly thereafter opened a small practice while working at Jacobi Hospital and teaching at the Albert Einstein College of Medicine.

Although no longer involved in formal research, I have over the years retained a steadfast interest in the concept of states of consciousness because it seems to provide a conceptual crossroad where the body meets the mind to give us a view of the person as a functioning whole. This holistic viewpoint is one I have endeavored to maintain, with varying success, in the clinical situation. I am convinced that, to understand our patients well, we must learn to pay equal attention to both body and mind, to both process and content, and to encourage the integration of just those parameters whose dissociation often lies at the very heart of severe pathology. I have tried, as clearly as I can, to elaborate this view in the pages that follow.

INTRODUCTION

Body–Mind Integration—
A Holistic Perspective

Even before I published my paper on the narcissistic state of consciousness (Bach, 1977), I had been engaged in piecemeal attempts to integrate in my own mind different ways of thinking about body and mind, subject and object, and process and content. I now believe that on some level all of us are continually engaged in a similar project, but that this effort becomes visible only when it is least successful, as happens with certain patients who are often consciously struggling to pull things together and make sense out of the disparate elements of their lives.

Although some of the chapters in this book were written for different occasions, they are all bound together by the particular viewpoint that I am espousing—a holistic or body–mind perspective. From this perspective, the psychoanalytic process can be viewed in both its spiritual and its animal aspects. To do less than to see the polarities of mind and body as a unity is, I believe, to severely distort elements of the human and the psychoanalytic situation. This unified vision is, after all, at the heart of the psychoanalytic effort as we try to do a close reading of the patient's words and feelings from an immediate empathic or subjective point of view, without losing sight of the larger objective, historical, and potential context.

If I reflect on psychosomatics as it was taught to me in the 1950s, it always seemed to incorporate some element of surprised discovery: learning that an established *physical* condition, such as gastric ulcers or immune response, might be affected by *psychological* variables, or that an established *psychological* condition, such as hysteria, might effect a change in the *physical* body. We have long since noticed that this categorization game leads down blind alleys, but it still somehow strains our everyday conceptual abilities to imagine that what we categorize as physical and what we categorize as mental may simply be views of a larger unity from different perspectives. This body–mind problem is, of course, linked to our difficulty dealing with the interdependence and interpenetration of subject and object or observer and observed, an issue that I touch on in chapter 4 as it relates to our understanding of human development and to the psychoanalytic situation.

For it is my firm conviction that as psychoanalysts we generally do better not to treat diagnostic conditions, or even particular symptoms, but that we work in the best interests of our patients by helping them to build or restore their own mental and physical regulatory and regenerative capacities. What these capacities are and how we go about helping to build or restore them is the subject matter of this book. I have generally tried to avoid elaborate theorizing and to concentrate instead on presenting a therapeutic attitude or frame of mind that incorporates and exemplifies the holistic vision I am trying to attain.

Changing our therapeutic frame of mind seems to involve, among other things, a change in the metaphors through which we view the analytic situation. In the early history of psychoanalysis great emphasis was placed on trauma and uncovering repressed secrets, which led to an investigative metaphor that viewed the analysis as a crime scene or natural catastrophe and the analyst as detective or archeologist. Later on, as experience accumulated, the emphasis shifted to the patient's resistance, which led to a military metaphor in which the analyst struggled against the patient's defenses and character armor. Still later, under the influence of object relations theorists, the analyst was seen more as a facilitator of growth, like a nanny or gardener, with images of hatching, holding, and unfolding and the transference as playground. More recently, the emphasis on mutuality and interdependence has promoted a systems metaphor in which the analyst is viewed as one part of a larger world that both influences and is influenced by him.

Although none of these metaphors are totally accurate, since they all emphasize certain aspects of the psychoanalytic situation while slighting or even obscuring other aspects, as long as they hold sway in the analyst's imagination they exert a powerful pressure on how he thinks and behaves with his patients. For example, the detective and military metaphors tend to highlight structure, content, and discontinuities like separation, whereas the nursing and systems metaphors tend to emphasize state, process, and continuities like attachment. Likewise the detective and military metaphors draw attention to boundaries, authority, and obedience; the gardener and systems metaphors tend to emphasize process, mutuality, and agency. In the detective and military metaphor there is a very clear demarcation between the observer and the observed or between the opposing forces; the nanny metaphor includes merging tendencies while the systems metaphor opts frankly for coconstruction and interdependence.

Since structure and state, content and process, continuity and discontinuity, obedience and agency, and interdependence and separateness all imply one another and are essential elements of life, it seems that, rather than selecting among them, one ought to look for some higher level of integration. But perhaps the main problem with some of these therapeutic metaphors is that they focus predominantly on the analyst and the analyst's goals, actions, and conceptualizations. The patient's goals and conceptualizations seem to have somehow been relegated to a secondary position, just as they so often are in certain areas of modern, fragmented, high-tech medical practice.

A Shift in the Analyst's Agency

Even if we have clear-cut convictions about the importance of the patient's role, the sacrifice of our own agency and *amour propre* is not an easy task, for the patient has come to us seeking help and thereby has endowed us with agency while often abnegating his own. If we are not to impose our agency on the patient's, we must be aware that the patient's agency is formed in the matrix of our response, a response that should be humanly consistent and humanely positive, that is, imperfectly loving. This shift of emphasis, from the analyst's agency to some form of mutuality, is one of the more difficult and puzzling aspects of psychoanalysis to which too little attention has been paid (Aron, 2001). This shift may seem paradoxical, for a patient might well ask, "Why do I come to you as an expert and pay you money only to be told that I must cure myself?" But perhaps the Delphic oracles were inspired when they treated their patients with conundrums, which the patients themselves were obliged to interpret and employ.

In any case, it was thoughts of this kind that led me to an increasing interest in the patient's raw experience or phenomenology, which may be expressed as an interest in the patient's states of consciousness. A state of consciousness seems to me a conceptual crossroad not only because it is defined by patterns of affect, body schema, thought organization, and self- and object awareness that integrate mental and physical parameters, but also because it seems that each person's "normal" or usual state of consciousness may embody his or her diagnostic classification. Thus one can speak of a hysterical state of consciousness, an obsessive-compulsive state of consciousness, or a narcissistic state of consciousness, which I attempted to define closely some time ago (Bach, 1977). In a certain sense one might envision psychoanalytic therapy as a process that can alter or modify a patient's normal state of consciousness, sometimes with uneven success along the multiple parameters.

Of course, we all experience fluctuations in our normal state of consciousness all the time, as when we are saddened or exhilarated or fatigued, intoxicated by alcohol, alerted by coffee, or engaged in sex, sports, watching TV, or sleeping. But when we speak of an altered state of consciousness we usually mean some more extreme and unusual variation as in a drugged state, a split-off multiple personality or a psychosis. Most of the time we keep trying to attain or maintain a state of consciousness that affords us a sense of well-being; that is, we try to achieve a balance among multiple parameters that feels comfortable. But sometimes, driven by special needs, we search for states that might not feel comfortable. An artist, for example, may seek to infuse the details of his experience with a kind of charged intensity of consciousness that might occasionally be painful, and certain sadists and masochists may do the same for reasons that we classify as pathological. I have discussed the sadomasochistic state of consciousness elsewhere (Bach, 1985, 1994) and continue this theme in chapter 8. Viewed from this perspective, sadomasochism differs from love in being an unsatisfactory attempt at finding an object with whom one might coexist in a state of mutual satisfaction; that is to say, sadomasochists have reached the stage of object choice but have not yet attained the stage of object love.

Trust in the Clinical Dyad

It was while I was grappling with the treatment of more disturbed narcissistic, sadomasochistic, and borderline patients that I developed the concept of "entering the patient's world" (Bach, 1985), that is, attuning oneself to the entire experienced world or the characteristic state of consciousness of a disturbed patient in order to understand him and to gain his trust. Doing so entails far more than what is usually meant by empathy. Ideally, it involves "meeting" (cf. Stern, 1998) not only the patient's parameters of emotional arousal but also his parameters of body schema and orientation, of thought and memory organization, and of self- and object awareness. By "meeting," I mean not necessarily attempting to match or regulate or yet deliberately change these parameters, but rather attempting to recognize and accept them and thereby bring them into a system of which the analyst forms a part. I believe that ultimately the analyst's attentive presence in this system does lead to increased trust and to mutual assimilation and interpenetration. I describe this kind of attention more particularly in chapters 1, 3, and 9. But while direct verbal communication may sometimes not be necessary to initiate important change, I believe that to understand consciously and eventually to formulate these changes in a verbal and symbolic manner always adds an *essential* extra dimension to a psychoanalysis.

For in a satisfactory analysis we are dealing not only with the individual states of consciousness of analyst and analysand but also with a mutually engendered and expanded (Tronick, 1998) or third (Winnicott, 1965; Ogden, 1985; Benjamin, 2004) state of consciousness. This enlarged state of consciousness in certain respects includes what Vygotsky (1978) has described as the zone of proximal development (ZPD), namely, the distance between the patient's current capabilities and his potential development with the assistance of the analyst. But I feel that the analyst's capabilities also are enhanced by the assistance of the patient, provided that a mutual sense of trust develops between them.

The development of this sense of trust in both patient and analyst has been a covert theme in the literature for many decades, and Ellman (1998, 2002) has recently begun to discuss it as analytic trust. For a while such concepts as therapeutic or working alliance seemed adequate, but as we analyzed more deeply regressed patients these terms began to feel too intellectual and too clearly extratransferential for the profound and cataclysmic forces with which we were dealing. Many of these patients did, indeed, seem to inhabit "other worlds" that we could never hope to reach, and, however intense our frustration at dealing with them, it seemed only a dim echo of their extreme despair at ever being able to reach us. Throughout this book I consider some of the transference and countertransference issues raised by this kind of work, as well as some of the more practical steps both patient and analyst might take to keep the strain from becoming unendurable.

For, indeed, in the depths of the transference–countertransference struggle that is conjured with these patients, we may be sorely tempted to abandon our psychoanalytic attitude, if not to abandon the patient, or else to question our fundamental tenets or our own ability to help. And this is why I believe that, when we are working with these patients, the daily mental hygiene of cleaning up or clearing the countertransference is a crucial task and that it is mandatory, even for the most experienced analyst, to have a confidant, peer group, or other outlet where he can fully and frankly discuss his feelings.

But the rewards of this mutual living-through accrue not only to the patient in his newly found ability to be alive in a world to which he may for the first time feel he belongs, but also to the analyst, who has been forced, despite himself, to deal throughout the analysis with his own characterological defects and basic faults. In the end, this mutual living-through renews the analyst's faith in the analytic process and provides one answer to the question of why we persist in doing such difficult work.

By examining what one does with the patient in the (sometimes long) intervals between making usable interpretations, I am trying to place an equal emphasis on the nonverbal and bodily interactions, as well as the verbal communications, between the two analytic participants. In his brilliant animal studies Hofer (2003) has analyzed the effects of catastrophic separation into its multiple components and demonstrated the hidden biological regulators of early attachment such as warmth and tactile, auditory, and vestibular stimulation. Of course, analysts have for a long time been providing their patients with such "hidden" psychobiological regulators as a couch, some pillows, a consistent schedule, a modulated sensory environment, and the like. I have tried to pay some attention to these factors and to show how they affect both patient and analyst in that most peculiar setting we call the psychoanalytic situation.

Finally, I believe that Freud was startlingly correct in his conclusion that the psychoanalytic cure is a cure effected by love—not only by the patient's love for the analyst but also by the analyst's love for the patient. In chapter 9, I discuss some of the reasons why it was difficult for Freud to admit this publicly, although he repeated it privately on many occasions, and even today this silence still prevails at most psychoanalytic institutes and in much of psychoanalytic discourse.

Motives ranging from the desire to include psychoanalysis among the quasi-medical reimbursable procedures to much larger issues involving the technicalization, fragmentation, and disenchantment of our culture and society have made it difficult to think about the place of love as a gestalt in psychoanalysis. Instead, we have tried to analyze love into its technical component parts, such as empathy, insight, affect regulation, holding, countertransference, and so on. While this attempt has often led to an increase in precision and understanding, it has sometimes resulted in a cookbook approach that leaves the student with all the ingredients except the one essential to bring them all together. In this respect, the infant researchers and baby watchers have often done better than we, for some of them seem to have kept in mind that the parameters they study in mothers and infants are the parameters of love. But, of course, they work in a field where sexuality is more diffuse and less threatening than in adult analysis.

In this book I have tried to be both analytic and synthetic; to pay attention to the smallest practical details, such as how we position the clock in the consulting room, as well as to the larger issues such as how we position our soul. For I believe that each person's life patterns are unique and meaningful to that person and that a patient's waking life, dream life, changing states of consciousness, and chronobiological rhythms all form a whole that we must try to grasp, attune to, and eventually love if we are ever to know each of our patients in the deepest possible way.

1

ON BEING FORGOTTEN AND
FORGETTING ONE'S SELF

But were I granted time to accomplish my work, I would not
fail to stamp it with the seal of that Time, now so forcibly
present to my mind, and in it I would describe men, even at
the risk of giving them the appearance of monstrous beings,
as occupying in Time a much greater place than that so spar-
ingly conceded to them in Space, a place indeed extended
beyond measure, because, like giants plunged in the years,
they touch at once those periods of their lives—separated by
so many days—so far apart in Time.
                    —Marcel Proust, *Remembrance of Things Past*

Although in the real world our experience of seeing, hearing,
smelling and touching people guarantees their existence for us,

---

In loving memory of Dr. Lester Schwartz.

their continued existence when not within the grasp of our senses is guaranteed only by our memory of them. And just as we keep people alive by remembering them, so we ourselves sustain our own feelings of aliveness not only through the ongoing awareness of our actual physical being but also by feeling that we exist and are remembered in the minds of others. This chapter is about those people who cannot feel continually alive in the present because as children they did not feel continually remembered and alive in the minds of their primary caretakers.

I first became interested in this topic when a patient, Jeffrey, mentioned that as a child he was well known at Macy's department store because his mother would regularly have to come to the lost-and-found department to retrieve him after she had lost him while shopping. Although Jeffrey recounted this as an amusing story, it turned out to be only the tip of an iceberg of isolation and despair of which he had remained largely unconscious.

From the beginning of the analysis I noted how often, after mentioning a name or incident, he would casually ask, "I've told you about him, haven't I?" or "Have I told you about that?" My countertransferential anxiety alerted me to the importance of these questions, but it took a while before we could discuss his belief that I really would not remember what he had said the day before or the day before that. It took even longer to bring out that when he returned to a subject from a previous meeting he often unconsciously tried subtly to remind me of the ground we had already covered so that I would be filled in even if I had entirely forgotten it.

The *Oxford English Dictionary* (1989) defines forgetting as "to miss or lose one's hold" on something or someone, and Jeffrey's conviction that he would be forgotten had led him to lose his hold on many things in his own life, most notably on a secure sense of himself.

Jeffrey presented with many phobias, one being a fear of flying. Since his executive position required him to fly on a fairly regular basis, he was constantly living with an anticipatory fear that at times would become so severe that he would walk off a plane he had already boarded. After an appreciable time in the analysis, when the transference had entered an early maternal phase, he began to get frightened on the couch; he would feel that he was drifting, had no direction, and become unable to think or talk. As these moments increased in intensity, he would often feel the necessity to sit up and look at me, which usually relieved his anxiety. Eventually it became clear that he was terrified of "losing his connection" with me and that sitting up and looking at me reassured him that I was still there and keeping him in mind. For many months we explored his anxiety about drifting without direction, and we learned that it culminated in a terrifying fantasy of falling endlessly into empty space. But we were still not sure what this fantasy was about.

When Jeffrey flew on business he was usually accompanied by Matthew, a young assistant whose career he had mentored and to whom he had a close attachment. We had both assumed that being accompanied by someone helped to reduce his anxiety, and, indeed, when frightened on the plane, Jeffrey often turned to Matthew for some kind of relief. But one day Matthew became ill shortly before their flight, and Jeffrey was obliged to fly without him. Much to our surprise, he discovered that he felt much better on the plane when Matthew was not with him "because I suddenly realized that even if I died there would be someone alive who would still remember me."

It thus became increasingly clear that at the heart of his many phobias and anxieties was a primary fear of being forgotten, a wordless fear of falling out of his mother's mind in an endless tumble into the oblivion of nonremembrance. This primary anxiety, which has been touched on in diverse ways in my own work (Bach, 1985, 1994), as well as in that of Winnicott (1965), Ogden (1985), and Modell (1990), among others, seems to be related to a disturbance in the capacity for evocative constancy and a consequent difficulty in the establishment of stable representations and reliable self- and object constancy (Auerbach, 1990, 1993). While the importance of a reliable maternal presence for the development of evocative constancy has often been noted, Jeffrey's case highlights the importance not only of the mother's physical presence, but especially of her psychic construction and holding the child in memory. In the next chapter I report, from the other side, as it were, the case of a mother whose repeated suicidal threats and attempts ended only when she became able to retain the memory of her children-with-herself-as-mother as part of an expanded state of consciousness. So this mutual holding in memory may well have life-and-death implications for both child and mother.

In Jeffrey's case, in addition to his fear of flying, he also suffered from an elevator phobia, a claustrophobia associated particularly with bathrooms, a fear of public speaking, and a generalized social phobia. As we analyzed each of these phobias in detail, we learned that they formed an interconnected network radiating from the same fear of being forgotten. Although we later began to use forgotten and not being remembered interchangeably, the phenomenological experience of the fear was of *not being remembered*.

And, indeed, that seemed an accurate enough assessment—for, with Jeffrey's mother at least, the state of not remembering her child seemed to be the more frequent and natural one, whereas forgetting him was often linked to her more deliberate but still unacknowledged withdrawal as punishment when Jeffrey had crossed her in some way. Phenomenologically for Jeffrey, being the Forgotten One still permitted an identity centered on himself, whereas not being remembered obliterated his self and shifted the center to the other person, as if the act of being remembered by someone were literally what was keeping Jeffrey alive.

Who actually was this mother who appeared to be, both in Jeffrey's memory and in our analytic reconstructions, someone who could not remember her own son? Here I should mention that I am not unaware of current controversies about childhood amnesia and reconstruction of the past (e.g., Fonagy, 1999), and I know that for a long time now it has been out of fashion to attend to Freud's (1919) admonition that "analytic work deserves to be recognized as genuine psycho-analysis only when it has succeeded in removing the amnesia which conceals from the adult his knowledge of his childhood from its beginning" (p. 183). Nonetheless, my clinical experience has repeatedly reinforced my belief that in many cases it is possible to reconstruct a patient's childhood with a reasonable degree of certainty and, moreover, that often the very process of this reconstruction is of great therapeutic importance.

Jeffrey's mother was still alive, and he continued to see her frequently; hence much of the material we worked on came from their telephone conversations or other interactions, often only a few hours or days old. Furthermore, Jeffrey's reports of his mother's current behavior and his recovered memories of her from his childhood showed a remarkable consistency over many years, and the understanding we eventually came to of her behavior allowed us to predict accurately what she would do in different and unfamiliar situations. Finally, as is typical in such cases, Jeffrey's initial conviction was that he had experienced the most normal of childhoods, that his siblings were all wonderfully content, and that his own symptoms and emerging childhood memories of confusion, pain, and despair were proof that there was indeed something terribly wrong with him.

Over the course of the analysis I indulged a fantasy that I was learning to understand Jeffrey's mother's psychology. This fantasy was based on the convergence of my two primary sources of information, Jeffrey's emerging memories of the interaction between himself and his mother and our own reenactments in the transference and countertransference in the course of the analysis. This process of coming to understand his mother involved a good deal of work, and its result was that Jeffrey now believed that he understood his mother's mind—a belief that is, I think, integral to his understanding of his own mind. Before that point in the analysis Jeffrey usually felt confused by his mother's mental operations and, indeed, quite hopeless about ever comprehending them. In the transference he was sometimes equally confused by my thinking, and it was very important that he come to understand not only how his mother's mind worked but also how my mind worked. I now believe that understanding how our mother's or father's mind operates belongs to the work of growing up but that this understanding has gone awry for many of our patients.

For example, when Jeffrey developed a serious medical condition that called for a decision about whether to opt for drug treatment or surgery, his mother urged surgery without even really listening to his explanation of the complex issues involved. By this time Jeffrey was able to see that she could not tolerate complexity or ambiguity and he could comment, "That's the way she is—she just does things and doesn't think about them and that way she can actually deny that anything really bad has happened!"

And, indeed, his mother, although an educated and intelligent woman, seemed to live in a world without ambiguity, complexity, or continuity, a world in which Jeffrey had been immersed to an extent that he had not fully comprehended. In his mother's world things were either good or bad, right or wrong, smart or stupid, friendly or dangerous. Nothing existed between these extremes; it was an either–or world. Furthermore, her children could find themselves in the smart or good category one moment and in the stupid or bad category the next without having any idea what they might have done to warrant this shift. What Jeffrey had experienced throughout his childhood and what he conveyed to me through transference enactments was that for his mother, and so for him in her world, there was no real concept of process. In practice this meant to Jeffrey that things could occur in extreme and arbitrary ways—if you sneezed that meant you were sick and going to die, or if you asked a question that meant you were stupid and didn't belong in the present company.

By paying attention to and reflecting on this uncertain and capricious world that Jeffrey inhabited with his mother, we slowly came to realize that one of its main characteristics was the pervasive absence of a sense of process. One day Jeffrey said,

> It seems to me that each time I meet my mother it's like having a new experience . . . as if we were starting afresh . . . I don't think I feel that way with most people . . . Sometimes I have a good conversation with her and I feel connected, but then I'll meet her again and it's almost like meeting a different person . . . I think that it's very upsetting to me . . . there's no continuity . . .

> When I was a kid, I used to take karate class . . . and I liked it a lot. The instructors there thought I was very good and they always picked me to demonstrate to the other kids. So I would be coming out of my karate class where they thought I was wonderful, and then I would be expecting her to pick me up. And she didn't come and I was waiting around wondering if she would come or not. And then I would start to have these fantasies about meeting some big guy on the street who insulted me and said I was only a kid and then I challenged him and used my karate and he was really amazed when I laid him out flat! . . . I guess I must have been real angry at my mother but then it never even crossed my mind . . .

> And I used to dream about coming out of karate class where everyone thought I was so wonderful and that my mother would be there and I would jump into the car and tell her how great the class was and she would be excited

along with me. . . . In my dreams it would all come together, the excitement of the class and my mother's excitement and everyone thinking I was great . . . But in reality it was always split apart.

And it was in just that way that we learned the details of the discontinuities in Jeffrey's life that had never been repaired, the ruptures that had never been mended, the rents in the fabric of his ego that brought him to a halt in whatever he might undertake, whether in work or in love. He seemed to live without the ordinary confidence that the past was connected to the present and would flow into the future and that each little piece of daily experience would fit into the overall pattern of a meaningful life.

On the contrary, when he first came to analysis Jeffrey's life was fragmented and was lived for the most part in discrete moments experienced as unconnected to each other in any meaningful way. Although he desperately felt the urge to make contact with other people, he could neither figure out how to do this nor manage somehow to pull together the scattered fragments of his life experience. Thus his memories of his life were split off from each other and stereotyped in such a way that living memories were covered by a screen of words. Emotional memories from his early years were almost entirely absent. One could say with some legitimacy that Jeffrey had forgotten his childhood.

I puzzled over that to myself for many months until one day Jeffrey came in angry with himself and began by saying,

J: I called my mother again . . . but why do I call her? Out of guilt or some other kind of obligation ? She kept asking me if I had written a thank-you note to this person I hardly know who did something or other for my brother that has nothing to do with me. . . . She's so concerned that I should do the right thing but she doesn't seem to have any idea about who I actually am . . . I can't understand why I keep calling her.

T: You keep calling her to make sure that she doesn't forget you.

J: [Seemingly taken aback] That makes a lot of sense. I never thought of it that way, but it's true. . . . Did I ever tell you that I always say, "Mom, it's Jeffrey," as if she wouldn't recognize my voice, wouldn't know who I am?

In fact, he had never told me this, but it dovetailed perfectly with his transference expectations that I would forget the things he told me and also with his subtle attempts to remind me about what had happened in our previous sessions. It made sense that Jeffrey would keep reminding his mother who he was and, expectably enough, at the height of this transference paradigm I occasionally found myself forgetting who the next patient was when the next patient was Jeffrey, whom I had been seeing at the same hour for years.

It was at this point that I began to realize more fully how we are bound together in time by a network of expectations of which we are dimly aware and that become clearly visible only when they are disrupted by dysfunction or pathology. I was reminded of a patient I had seen many years before who would regularly ask me, "When you come into the waiting room, how can you be so sure that it's me who will be there and not another person or some giant insect or a plant?" Although at the time I was able to respond in an appropriately analytic way, it now seemed to me that I hadn't fully appreciated the depth of anxiety and uncertainty that was expressed in that poignant cry of doubt.

While I had assumed from early on that there must be some kind of projective identification going on between Jeffrey and his mother that made her forget him, over time we began to learn things about his mother that made her own part in this equation loom even larger than expected. For as Jeffrey began to feel less need to call his mother so frequently, it became evident that she felt no need at all to call him. And so they went from speaking to each other several times a week to not talking to each other for weeks on end until Jeffrey called her, at which point she would reproach him for not having called sooner. His mother was apparently unable even to entertain the possibility that she might have called him.

I now learned that when Jeffrey was at college his father died and his mother had not even notified him beforehand of his father's illness. She had called him to return for the funeral only at the last minute so as "not to disturb his studies." In the period of mourning following his father's death she spoke only of her own loss, never once even acknowledging that Jeffrey also had lost someone important to him. And when it came time to distribute some of his father's legacy which had been left entirely to her, she divided it in such a way that Jeffrey was clearly deprived of his fair share.

But, of course, the most significant consequences of his feeling not remembered by his mother were his pervasive sense that *he was an unworthy and unmemorable person* and his own inability to vividly remember his childhood and so have a past. By not remembering his childhood he was forgetting a very important dimension of himself, and one that not only existed in the past but that also was unconsciously affecting his every thought and action in the present as well as his hopes and aspirations for the future.

In his repeated references to the concept of *Nachträglichkeit,* Freud (1896) insisted on the continual two-way interaction between past and present. He noted not only the delayed effects of trauma, but also the mind's capacity retrospectively to attribute a causal meaning to the past. In this way both the past and the present are constantly reorganizing and retranscribing each other in human memory in ways that clearly influence our expectations and have crucial importance in shaping our futures.

It was this vital and sensual world of his childhood that Jeffrey had lost, and it began to emerge in bits and fragments only as the analysis proceeded. In the course of our explorations, I repeatedly sensed that Jeffrey's amnesia with respect to his childhood was in some way connected for him to his experience of not being remembered by his mother and that the memories he was recovering in analysis were continually reorganizing themselves around his experience of being remembered by me.

It was then that I realized that a person's memories and experiences are like individual beads; only when they are strung together to become a necklace do they achieve continuity and a gestalt form. The string on which they are assembled is the child's sense of his own continuous existence in the mind of the parent, where the beads of experience are strung together and become the necklace of a connected life. We know, for example, that many people whose parents were actively involved with them but took a primarily negative view of things tend to string their experiences on a negative filament so that each new experience is assembled and viewed from its negative aspect. But the most difficult therapeutic issues arise in those cases where the parent was emotionally absent or uninvolved, for then the string of continuity for assembling experience is missing, and the child is left clutching a handful of beads or memories that form no discernible pattern. This experience feels similar to the momentary shock many of us have had when a necklace or bracelet suddenly breaks and what had been a coherent whole or gestalt a moment before suddenly becomes a confusion of disconnected parts colliding and rolling every which way on the floor.

But such was consistently Jeffrey's experience as a child, for he said about his mother, "It's not that she wasn't there, but I just couldn't feel any real connection to her!" It then became clear to me that what was missing was the string of emotional connection and the continuity in time on which the beads of his experience could be strung.

So it seems that the mind creates our experiential world by both connecting and transforming experience across time. If, for example, we project a motion picture strip at 10 frames per second, we see a series of static, disconnected images, but when we project it at 24 frames per second these discrete images suddenly turn into a flow of continuous, connected movement or action. While this may tell us something about the processing speed of the brain center that establishes visual motion, it also suggests that a certain frequency over time is necessary for a visual sense of continuity to become established. This phenomenon coincides with the experience of many analysts that a certain frequency of sessions is essential for the establishment of a deep transference, especially with those patients for whom problems of attachment, separation, and continuity are foremost.

I have also come to believe that with such patients it is primarily the analyst's faith, trust, hope, and concern—that is, his emotionally charged remembering of the patient—that keeps the patient connected to him and to the analysis. By this I mean that, if a dismembered life is to come together, the analyst must keep the patient continually alive in his own mind, and the patient must believe that the analyst holds him and keeps him alive in memory. Reciprocally, of course, the patient must learn to keep the analyst consistently alive and the analyst must feel that he remains alive in the mind of the patient. This seems to be an important condition for what we know as love.

Now, by reaffirming the importance of this mutual holding in memory, I do not mean to slight the importance of the array of defensive operations, denials, withdrawals, and attacks on linking that figure so prominently in all patients and also, I believe, in all analysts. As I have discussed elsewhere (Bach, 1985), these defensive operations are often most clearly visible at times of separation or reattachment, such as at the end of a vacation, when the patient's reluctance to reengage closely may often be paralleled by the analyst's difficulties reengaging. For it can also be, among other things, a burden and a worrisome responsibility for parent and child to hold each other closely in mind—witness the presence not only of pain but also of mutual liberation when children finally do leave home. For these and many other reasons, along with the need and desire to be remembered by the parent, there is also always a need to forget and be forgotten, to be released from the bonds of memory, to soar to the freedom of independence or sink into the oblivion of sleep.

This need to be left alone, to be forgotten and to forget was not absent in Jeffrey. His persistent fear that I might forget him was, at another level, countered by the compulsive wish that I would completely forget him and leave him alone and unencumbered by my insistent presence. In the first few years of the treatment he would sometimes sink into a state where he would stop talking; he would respond to my questions by saying there was nothing on his mind and that he was unable to locate any feeling other than apathy and a painful sense of being utterly disconnected from everyone. These silent and disconnected states could last for much of the hour, and it was very difficult to relate them to what had been going on moments before or to help Jeffrey deal with them. Over time these silences grew shorter and shorter; a silence that might have lasted 15 minutes in the first year became only a momentary lapse in his continual stream of consciousness.

At first during these silences I experienced a kind of apathetic disconnection myself; it seemed that the countertransference was not providing its usual cues about what might be going on. In the available time—of which I had plenty—I would force myself to entertain hypotheses about concealed rage, murderous intent, attacks on linking, reunion with the dead mother, and other interesting thoughts, but eventually I came to believe that I was simply trying to keep myself and Jeffrey artificially alive with these speculations and that I might do better to join him in the land of the dead. This was not an easy task because it felt very uncomfortable there, but it gave me some experience of what it must have been like for Jeffrey to exist for most of his childhood in this desolate terrain of unconnected beings. Indeed, in this Dantesque landscape, momentary outbursts of anger seemed to come as a welcome relief, which led me to believe that Jeffrey's whole family system had achieved its moribund condition only by draining itself almost entirely of aggressive and libidinal energies.

So, although Jeffrey's stuporous states were in one way a simple repetition of the disconnection that had existed between him and his parents, they were in another way a participatory reenactment of the family defenses against the anger and violent feelings that are necessary for separation-individuation. It seemed that, just as his mother had held the power of psychological life and death over Jeffrey throughout his childhood, he was now, through his silence, enacting that power of psychological life and death over me and over the analysis. But finally, and, perhaps most important, these silences constituted an avoidance of the mourning and reparation that might have led to more mature and more genuine experiences of connection. I cannot elaborate here how this was replicated and eventually also worked through in the transference.

As I think about all this, it seems to me that one way of summarizing what I learned is to say that *a parent can actually destroy a child, both psychically and physically, by not carrying or holding that child's memory or representation in a particular way.* Conversely, as the child becomes an adult and the generational power reverses, the adult child may now destroy the parent by not carrying that parent's memory in a particular way. For, while coming of age always involves some form of destruction of the parent (Loewald, 1980), it makes a huge difference to the parties involved whether the parental psyche is left fragmented and dislocated in the universe or whether the parent can mourn his or her own aging while nevertheless rejoicing in the continuity of the generations in which his own life now finds a diminishing place.

So it seems that in normal development there is a kind of mutual holding in memory from the beginning that is of defining importance to both parent and child and can be seen in the mother's jubilation when the child first seems to recognize her, and her disappointment when he does not. We know now that infants can recognize their mother's scent within 24 hours; this mutual recognition and holding seem to be in place from early on. We can imagine that, with a normal baby, the mother's *expectation* of being recognized and her ability to provide the appropriate stimulation play an important role in bringing about this recognition, and that an apathetic mother might take much longer to engage and activate this mutual memory system. Somewhere along this continuum lie the intermittently engaged mother, the depressed mother, and, at the extreme, the missing mother and Spitz's (1965) marasmus and infant death. Marasmus can be viewed as demonstrating that the infant's need to hold and be held in memory is life sustaining; one might view Jeffrey's plight metaphorically as a form of intermittent marasmus.

Of course, even in normal development a certain kind of destruction is not entirely avoided; such controlled destruction must take place over and over on each developmental level for mature object relationships to evolve. That is to say, connection cannot exist without the disconnection that destroys it, and normal remembering cannot exist without forgetting, as Borges (1962) has so beautifully shown in his story about a man who was unable to forget anything.

Cognitive researchers have recently begun to demonstrate a similar phenomenon (Nader, Schafe, and LeDoux, 2000). It has been known for some time that memory formation, which is fixed by protein synthesis, can be disrupted if a drug that inhibits protein synthesis is given within six hours of the memory stimulus. But apparently even after a memory has become fixed, if the stimulus to recall it is reproduced and the memory reactivated, it returns to a malleable state and can once more be disrupted if protein synthesis is inhibited. What that seems to mean is that fixed memory is capable of becoming malleable again when exposed to the original memory stimulus, and thus events in the present can influence even fixed memories of the past. Of course, this latest scientific discovery can be seen as a confirmation of Freud's (1896) concept of *Nachträglichkeit,* and of the continual flux and interchange he postulated between the past, present, and future and between remembering and forgetting. But how does this affect the problem that concerns us here—Jeffrey's difficulties with his sense of process, continuity, and being remembered?

We know that in normal development the mother is the keeper of the child's memories and that she normally inserts little bookmarks into the memory stream by saying, "Yesterday we went to the playground and saw the little black dog," or "Do you remember last month when we went to Grandma's house? Well, tomorrow we're going again." Thus she becomes the loom or matrix of the child's past, present, and future by helping to reintegrate memories at each higher level of development. By stringing events on the filament of his mother's presence, the child creates a sense of himself as an enduring and expanding existence over time. Simultaneously, the child is influencing the mother's memory, quickening it with the vivid verbal and sensual details that are so characteristic of the normal mother–toddler dyad.

In his normal everyday experience the child is incidentally learning concepts for configuring such experience as the simultaneity and succession of events and notions of time that will form the very fabric of his working ego. The importance of this implicit knowledge is difficult to overestimate; we take it so much for granted, but it is underscored when we turn to pathology such as Jeffrey's where the interaction with the mother, instead of leading to the synthesis and integration of events over time, leads instead to fragmented experiences.

Jeffrey was very prone to losing or misplacing things. He would finish a report and then not be able to locate it, misplace his keys or his wallet, lose an important letter, or mislay the TV remote control. His assistant spent a considerable amount of time searching for the many things that Jeffrey had misplaced. Analyses of these parapraxes as well as of similar parapraxes in the transference consistently brought us back to some real or fantasized lack of connection with his mother or me, thereby confirming Anna Freud's (1967) dictum that children who chronically lose things "live out a double identification, passively with the lost objects which symbolize themselves, actively with the parents whom they experience to be as neglectful, indifferent, and unconcerned toward them as they themselves are toward their possessions (p. 16).

Of course, habitually losing things and the experience of feeling lost were only the more obvious aspects of a state of intermittent inner fragmentation with which Jeffrey had lived from early childhood. I often puzzled about how he could have reached maturity and such a high executive position while at the same time feeling so lost and experiencing himself as so insignificant. He was very intelligent, his chronic feelings of stupidity notwithstanding, but he was definitely an underachiever in many areas. He had successfully walked through all his schooling in a mental fog, immediately forgetting most of what he had learned. He seemed to have excellent instincts for doing the right thing interpersonally or on the job.

But he lived in constant terror of being asked to explain why he did what he did because he could not link things together in a synoptic or coherent way or feel he had an overview that would allow him to give an account. Thus, despite his intelligence, learning something new in any area filled him with dread because he could not imagine a learning process over time and because he felt he lacked the ability to conceptualize it or to connect it with previously learned information.

I came to realize about Jeffrey, and the many other patients I have seen like him, that his sense of time had become fragmented, so that all too often the whole world was experienced in bits and pieces, none of which had any meaning. For a sense of meaning arises out of the connectedness of things and their relationship to each other in time; when the links of this connectedness are broken, then we are left with only empty moments in a frightening and meaningless void. And I knew then that Jeffrey had been driven into his stuporous states as an escape from this terrifying sense of meaninglessness. A phrase from Shakespeare came to mind about Macbeth murdering Sleep. And I thought that, by not carrying or holding a child's memory or representation in a connected way, a parent can actually murder Time for that child and leave him with all the resulting cognitive and emotional difficulties that I have tried to describe.

This particular story has a happy ending, for Jeffrey did eventually learn how to learn, how to connect without too much fear, and how to overcome many of the deficits he had been left with. It was only as I finished writing this chapter that I remembered that, when he was engaged to be married, the first present Jeffrey gave his fiancée was a watch—the significance of which completely escaped me at the time.

2
NARCISSISM REVISITED

As we revisit narcissism in the 21st century, it may be instructive to recall that 35 years ago in America, students of narcissism were fiercely divided between those analysts who viewed the narcissistic disorders in terms of conflict and those who viewed them in terms of deficit, and that some analysts' professional careers were decisively influenced by which theory they espoused. In retrospect, with the passage of time and as we have come to understand that conflicts and deficits entail one another, this controversy now seems emblematic of the either–or thinking that characterizes the narcissistic disorder itself in its efforts to deal with the polarities of human life. At that time I suggested that the either–or thinking and the alternations between self and object that are so characteristic of pathological narcissism are related to a pervasive disruption of integrated self-awareness and are accompanied by experiences of narcissistic disequilibrium (Bach, 1977).

I used as a classic example of disrupted self-awareness the report of one patient who said that when she was having sex with her

boyfriend, "I can't make the smooth transition. . . . I'm either me, totally me and so excited that nothing else exists, or else I'm Tony's
lover, and I can give him pleasure, but then I don't have any myself."
While people normally seem capable of integrating the transition
between subjective awareness (i.e., being "totally me") and objective self-awareness (i.e., being totally "Tony's lover"), people with
narcissistic disorders, as a result of conflicts and failures in early
development, lack the ability to seamlessly integrate these two perspectives on the self. The consequences of these failures of integration are manifold and include disturbances of self- and object
representations, disturbances of cognitive processing and agency,
and, ultimately, disruptions in work and love.

These problems of structural integration find expression in dynamic fantasies that are among the most fascinating aspects of
narcissism. I have discussed these at length elsewhere (Bach,
1985, 1994), so I will mention only some typical self-state fantasies. They include the fantasy of the narcissistic cocoon, which iso-
lates the patient from both his external and internal worlds;
fantasies of implosion and explosion, which deal with regulating
narcissistic equilibrium; fantasies about a double, an imaginary
companion, a wise baby, or an androgyne, which deal with selfobjects and idealized objects; or fantasies of escape into another
world, which deal with transcendence. Above all, there are the
sadomasochistic fantasies, which deal with all these themes but
especially with the narcissist's ultimate *despair* at ever being able to
acknowledge or gratify his dependent longings or to engage in a relationship of mutuality. These themes of sadomasochistic relations
and perversions are not only of clinical importance, but they are
also rooted in the great polarities of psychic life, such as self and
other, subjectivity and objectivity, attachment and separation, activity and passivity, and pleasure and unpleasure. The narcissist
and sadomasochist have great difficulty integrating these polarities, and they attempt to deal with them by either–or thinking and
by an acting out that effectively suppresses one of the polarities
rather than uniting or integrating them.

In the past few decades a whole generation of baby watchers,
neuroscientists, cognitive scientists, and attachment researchers
have presented us with invaluable data about the deficits and
conflicts of early development that may lead to an inability either
to integrate or to sustain multiple perspectives on self and other.

This research has been amply reviewed and integrated in a number of outstanding publications (e.g., Coates, 1998; Main, 2000; Fonagy et al., 2002; Slade, 2004; Beebe and Lachmann, 2005), and I can simply add my conclusion that for the most part these data correlate remarkably well with clinical observations on adults. Thus this research, coupled with my own observations over time, has confirmed my impression that many instances of disrupted self-awareness in adult patients are traceable to disruptions of communication that began in the early mother–infant dyad and continued as a cumulative trauma throughout childhood.

For it seems that infants seek attachments that will help to create a world by ordering time and space and allow them to adequately organize and satisfy their inborn needs and capacities. Out of these interactions between genetic potential and environmental response arise, depending on our perspective, the drives, affects, internal representations, and thoughts that become meaningfully organized to constitute the infant's world.

It seems that meaning and trust originate in the early months as the mother begins to feel what the baby is feeling and the baby begins to feel what the mother is feeling; that is, meaning and trust arise in the reliably consistent interpenetration and mutual regulation of affects and gestural communications in the early dyad. Out of this good-enough mutuality the baby develops the capacity to feel both connected to others and yet separate, which is the dialectical paradox of development. These larger issues of attachment and separation, or relatedness and self-identity, are mirrored endopsychically in states of consciousness, so that the state of subjective awareness, or "being totally me and so excited that nothing else exists," proclaims an experience of being a vital and alive separate agent, whereas the state of objective self-awareness, or "being Tony's lover," proclaims an experience of being an object for another human being to whom one is attached.

When I first encountered these phenomena, I realized that narcissistic pathology implies a deficit in switching or integration, a difficulty in moving between the perspective of seeing and feeling oneself at the center of the universe and the perspective of seeing and feeling oneself as just one more self among many others. Ultimately, I distinguished two versions of narcissistic pathology: the overinflated and the deflated types (Bach, 1985, 1994). The *overinflated,* grandiose, hypomanic, and sadistic narcissist consciously experiences himself as the center of the world and tries to form a mirroring transference in which the analyst is expected to reflect and reinforce the patient's grandiosity. The *deflated,* depressed, clinging, and masochistic narcissist, on the other hand, consciously experiences himself as insignificant in relation to other people, and he tries to form an idealizing transference in which the analyst is expected to embody everything the patient cannot hope to be. Each of these pathological types seems to have made an either–or choice: the overinflated narcissist has chosen to increase his sense of vitality, aliveness, and selfhood at the expense of impoverishing his object relations, whereas the deflated narcissist has chosen to cling to his objects at the expense of feeling his own aliveness, separateness, and self-worth. Eventually, for each type the analysis uncovers the other side of the coin; that is, it uncovers the helpless, dependent, and masochistic elements in the overinflated type and the grandiose and sadistic elements in the deflated type and thus enables a better integration.

For a while it was a puzzle to me why these patients seemed obliged to make this unfortunate choice between *either* maintaining their own selfhood and separateness *or else* being attached and related to others. This was in the late 1950s and early 1960s, and I was just becoming acquainted with the works of Winnicott and the early Kohut, which seemed to be most relevant to what I was observing. Having been trained as a psychologist, I first began to explore systematically the narcissistic thought disorder and eventually to conceptualize the narcissistic state of consciousness. I described in detail how the lived experience of the narcissistic patient is dramatically different from normal experience with regard to language and thought organization, affect regulation, the sense of agency and the experience of time, space and causality (Bach, 1977). This work seemed useful not only to sharpen diagnostic criteria, but also because I felt that understanding the world in which the patient lived enabled the analyst to enter the patient's affective and phenomenal world and to be there with him, a position that seemed to me a prerequisite for any serious attempt at analysis.

I could see that these patients tended to be desymbolized (Freedman and Berzofsky, 1995), overly abstract or concrete (Akhtar and Thomson,1982), intolerant of ambiguity, and unable to accept multiple points of view, especially the point of view of their analyst. Following Winnicott, I began to think of them as being unable to construct or to utilize transitional space. And, indeed, it seemed that once they began to use the analyst as a transitional object and to establish transitional space, they slowly became better able to deal with the gradient complexities of actual life and real object relationships.

Because my point about the cognitive and emotional limitations in narcissism has been frequently misunderstood, let me insert a brief example. I once knew a manic-depressive patient who in his manic phase used to call me Dr. 3B, or Doctor Bach/Beethoven/Brahms. I took this as an illustration of Freud's (1915b) concept of a loss of thing cathexis; only very mobile word-cathexes remained, sometimes verging on "word salad." I should mention also the typical case of a high-functioning, narcissistic CEO who idealized his wife until she needed surgery, which for him destroyed her perfection, whereupon he immediately replaced her with another idealized woman. That is an example of interchangeable object cathexes rather than word cathexes, but this same executive was also an inveterate liar, so that in many instances word cathexes were also interchangeable. It seemed that some deep emotional attachment, whether to people or to words, was lacking in both cases.

I noticed that, in addition to cognitive deficits, these patients also suffered from severe emotional dysregulation, which inclined toward the hypomanic in the overinflated types and toward the depressive in the deflated types, but could also vary sharply and unpredictably. Indeed, it often seemed as if their emotional thermostats were malfunctioning or nonexistent, which was consistent with their overall problems of self- and mutual regulation. For a long time we have wondered about the criteria for distinguishing narcissistic affect dysregulation from major depressive or bipolar disturbances. But it remains my impression that there is a continuum with considerable overlap and that a great many people with analytically treatable narcissistic disorders are still being diagnosed as unipolar or bipolar and treated only with medication, which may help their behavior but not their basic regulatory issues or their problems with relating to others.

Fortunately, when these patients do get into a good analysis where they begin to trust the analyst and become able to use him or her as a transitional or selfobject, then they often become emotionally and cognitively regulated, with or without medication.

When I first began to see this consistently happen, many years ago, I could find only the pioneering studies of Spitz (1945, 1965) and Mahler (1963) and the theorizing of Ferenczi (1932), Winnicott (1945, 1953, 1955), Kohut (1959, 1966), and Balint (1968) to help me understand this striking phenomenon. Nowadays, of course, thanks to the enormous efforts of the infant and attachment researchers (Tronick et al., 1978; Beebe and Lachmann, 2005), we have stop-action films and minutely recorded observations showing very similar effects in the well-regulated maternal dyad, and also a multitude of observations about potential causes of disruption in the dysregulated dyad. To speak of a match, a mismatch, a repair, and then a reattunement has become commonplace, whether we are referring to a mother–infant dyad or an enactment in adult analysis.

Indeed, the extensive research in the attachment literature seems to suggest that early attachment patterns may be largely environmental in origin (Main, 2000), and it seems likely that what we analysts, observing from the inside, have termed the narcissistic disorders are in as yet unclear ways closely connected to what the infant researchers, observing from the outside, have seen as early patterns of attachment difficulties.

A significant attempt to link these two observational stances is the Adult Attachment Interview (George, Kaplan, and Main, 1984, 1985, 1996), a protocol in which adults are asked to describe and reflect on their relationships with both parents as well as their own experiences of rejection, separation and loss in childhood. When parents take this interview it turns out to be highly predictive of the attachment patterns of their children, even if they take the interview before their children are born. Most interestingly, what correlates with secure attachment patterns in their children is not the actual degree of trauma in the parents' own childhood but, rather, the parents' ability to talk about the events of their childhood in an open, reflective, and nondefensive way. Thus the parents' ability to achieve objective or reflective self-awareness about themselves and their own childhood has now been demonstrated to be a substantial predictor of their children's overt behavior in early childhood. So the available research has only confirmed my experience that, with certain qualifications, a great many cases of disrupted awareness or reflexivity in adults are traceable to disruptions of communication beginning in the early dyad and continuing as a cumulative trauma throughout childhood. Where I differ technically with some analysts is in my strong belief that not only should these early parent–child interactions be analyzed as they recur in the here-and-now transference, but also that the recovery and the revivification of childhood memories is still an important, if not an essential, part of our work.

In general, narcissistic and borderline patients have greater than usual difficulties in establishing a sense of self as agent and in acquiring the reflective awareness to view this self in the context of other selves. Thus they have related difficulties with self–other differentiation, with appropriate boundaries, and with accurately reading and understanding their own minds or the minds of others. Many of these difficulties are connected to the developmental paradox of being born out of someone's flesh yet becoming separate from that person, of being attached to other people yet having one's individual identity, of being able to live in one's own subjectivity yet also able to observe oneself from the outside like a stranger.

Psychoanalysis responded to these paradoxes with Freud's discovery of the transference and his concept of the transference as a playground (Freud, 1914, p. 154), with Winnicott's (1953) concept of transitional objects and a transitional space that belongs to everyone and no one, with Kohut's (1966, 1971) formulations about selfobjects, and with Klein's (1946) projective identification in which mental contents are mutually exchanged. In fact, the history of psychoanalysis itself may be viewed as a prolonged, if sometimes unsuccessful, attempt to maintain an appropriate tension between analyzing or deconstructing the elements of psychic life and linking or integrating them.

I have emphasized that narcissistic patients have great difficulty in constructing or using transitional space, which is one way of thinking about them. From a slightly different perspective, I saw these patients as having problems of evocative constancy, that is, having a weakened capacity to hold on to the object representation when the object is absent, or to hold on to the self-representation when the object is not there to reflect and reinforce it. Thus the overinflated narcissist is someone whose grasp on his objects is fading and who, like the Marquis de Sade (Bach and Schwartz, 1972), compensates by overinflating himself and insisting he is so powerful that he does not need any objects and can even destroy them. The deflated narcissist, on the other hand, is someone whose cathexis of his own self is fading and who, like Sacher Masoch, compensates by overinflating an idealized object and masochistically clinging to that object for security. It began to seem clearer that the thinking and affective organization characteristic of narcissism must inevitably lead to sadomasochistic object relations, since the either–or thinking, desymbolized concreteness, lack of object constancy, intolerance for ambiguity, and inability to perceive multiple points of view all conspired to make mutuality impossible. These observations, coming out of my primary concern with narcissism, led me to an increasing interest in sadomasochism, the perversions, and sadomasochistic object relationships.

Although actual sexual perversions may be met with more often than one might suppose, sadomasochistic relationships in the larger sense are extremely common in everyday life and practice. While they may or may not include perversions, they always include conscious or unconscious sadomasochistic fantasies, the prototype of which is the beating fantasy. In my view, actual perversions and sadomasochistic object relations are connected because both arise as a defense against and an attempt to repair some traumatic loss that has not been adequately mourned, and that the reparative process importantly involves recognizing and mourning that loss (Bach and Schwartz, 1972; Bach, 1991). While this loss may occur at any stage of development, it may include not only loss of love but also loss of the self through childhood illness, traumatic disillusionment, overwhelming anxiety, and so forth. It also often includes the loss or absence of an adequate maternal or paternal figure.

For, as Kris (1984) has helped clarify, these patients are very often struggling with *divergent* conflicts of ambivalence that involve the most basic polarities of life, such as holding or abandoning objects, loving or hating, being active or passive and sadistic or masochistic, to name a few. For these patients *at this stage* the mutative process is often not verbal interpretation of drive-defense or *convergent* conflicts, but rather a prolonged process of mourning and reintegration that entails a mindful interpenetrative oscillation between these polarities rather than a defensive splitting (see chapter 5).

As Kris (1984) has noted, "a process akin to mourning bears the relationship to the (divergent) conflicts of ambivalence that remembering, through lifting of repression, bears to the (convergent) conflicts of defense" (p. 220). This process is facilitated by the analyst's holding, framing, synthesizing, and metabolizing projections, and eventually it leads to a more organized state where interpretations of convergent conflicts become usable. The separation is nowhere nearly as neat as I have pictured, and, because trauma becomes part of an intrapsychic conflict (Eagle, 1984; Busch, 2005), certain convergent conflicts related to trauma may appear alongside divergent ones at an early stage, whereas certain divergent conflicts may persist throughout much of the analysis.

In the course of the mourning that regulates and diminishes these conflicts, the patient typically mourns the loss of his own omnipotence, of good objects, of lost potential, and of his capacity to love and to hate in a useful way, all of which are encapsulated in the losses and insufficiencies of the current transferential relationship with the analyst. While these losses recapitulate for the patient the losses inherent in his painful early relationships, they also include losses specific to the current relationship and to the analyst's real personal deficiencies, which become acutely actualized in the transference–countertransference communications.

With regard to managing the depression that arises from mourning and confronting loss, we have much to learn from Hofer's (2003) brilliant animal studies in which he has analyzed catastrophic separation into its multiple component parts and demonstrated the "hidden" biological regulators of early attachment, such as the mother's provision of warmth and tactile, auditory, and vestibular stimulation. He notes that every separation or transition means the "loss of a number of individual regulatory processes that were hidden within the interactions of the previous relationship, with individual components of the interaction regulating specific physiological and behavioral systems" (pp. 194–195). Fortunately, this research also suggests that the catastrophic depressive reactions resulting from the simultaneous loss of multiple "hidden" regulators may sometimes be partially reversed by reprovision of some of the individual regulatory components that were offered by the lost relationship.

In this regard, analysts have for decades been providing their patients with "hidden" psychobiological regulators such as a couch, some pillows and a soothing sensory environment. In my own practice I usually try to adjust the consulting room to each patient's preferences about temperature, ventilation, sound, lighting, pillows, blankets, furniture arrangement, and so forth, within the bounds of my possibilities; when a change cannot be made because it is too trying for me or even impossible, then I give a clear explanation. This policy applies to scheduling as well, which I try to keep flexible if I can do so without generating too much countertransference, a dilemma that can also be discussed. Some patients simply need a longer time to get started, and I try to accommodate them whenever possible, within my own limitations. I also arrange for the clock to be visible both to the patient and to me, so that we can share this information. Many of these apparently inconsequential adjustments of the analytic environment may be thought of as paralleling the hidden biological regulators of early attachment such as the warmth, texture, and tactile, auditory, and vestibular stimulation that Hofer has so brilliantly described.

Being in tune with the patient's physical as well as mental being is, of course, much simpler when we are part of the system along with the patient, and this happens automatically from the start as we attempt to meet the parameters of his ongoing state of consciousness. At the beginning with a more disturbed patient we rarely find a unified transference configuration, but rather a series of fragmentary and disorganized transference reactions that may sometimes oscillate between extremes and may feel confusing to both patient and analyst. As the treatment progresses, we often see the classic selfobject paradigms emerging that Kohut (1971) so vividly described. It may in fact take considerable time for even a primitive selfobject transference to emerge with some stability, but with enough patience this eventually happens, even with the most disturbed patients.

At this time, as throughout the treatment, there are often oscillations between rupture and subsequent repair of the relationship. If rupture and repair may be viewed as the polarities between which any relationship or therapeutic process alternates, then trust can be seen as the essential lubricating medium within which these oscillations occur. As Winnicott (1956) reminded us, "The first ego organization comes from the experience of threats of annihilation which do not lead to annihilation and from which, repeatedly, there is *recovery*. Out of such experiences confidence in recovery begins to be something which leads to an ego and to an ego capacity for coping with frustration" (p. 304). Especially with these challenging patients it helps to remember that rage may sometimes be the only organizing force available to them, and that rage often covers the most profound feelings of shame and humiliation that arise when any close contact with another human being is attempted. In this connection we know that attachment to the treatment is our primary goal and that, while remaining within the patient's world is the road to attachment, making an "objective" comment or interpretation from outside is usually the road to separation. At the beginning, with these "unclassical" patients, the road to separation should be taken only when there is clear reason to do so. In the ordinary course of events a patient will eventually begin to take distance on his own subjectivity and to develop reflective self-awareness, which can then be taken as one sign that interpretations have now become usable.

In the meantime, however, we are sometimes faced with some variety of developing sadomasochistic transference in which either the patient begins to feel persecuted and trapped in the analysis or the analyst begins to feel persecuted by the patient's resistance or rage. When this happens we have reached the level of the sadomasochistic beating fantasy so frequently found with more disturbed patients. This fantasy serves both a defensive and compensatory function. It links the couple in such a way that the masochist is unconsciously saying, "Do anything you want to me—beat me or kill me if you must—but don't ever leave me," whereas the sadist is replying, "I can do anything I want to you—I can beat you or torture you forever—but you'll never be able to leave me!" Both fantasies feed on the denial of permanent loss, which is essentially the denial of the original trauma. Both the narcissist and the sadomasochist, who are often the same person, find it enormously difficult to give up their original objects precisely because these objects have been so traumatic or unsatisfying and the trauma has never been adequately mourned or worked through. In this way they seem to resemble avoidant and ambivalent infants who, in the Strange Situation,[1] either cannot display the appropriate emotions or else cannot resolve them.

---

[1]The Strange Situation is a standardized laboratory procedure involving two separations and reunions between the caregiver and the infant (see Ainsworth et al., 1978).

You have probably noted that we are dealing here with part-objects or selfobjects or projectively identified objects—that is, that the narcissist and the sadomasochist are primarily using their objects in a functional way with little or no consideration for that object's own intrinsic needs. It has been repeatedly observed that these patients experience themselves as having been used in this instrumental way in their own childhood and that, indeed, this is the only way they know of relating to other people or to themselves. This experience of being used predominantly as someone else's narcissistic or part-object may have been openly communicated or conveyed only in an implicit relational way, but it is often denied or unconscious when the patient comes for treatment, and it may at first surface only in transference enactments. As the patient begins to use the analyst in this narcissistic way and the analyst lends himself to this usage while elastically maintaining the overall framework, we begin to see the development of analytic trust, of a transitional area, and of mutual regulatory processes.

Although at first the overinflated narcissist may be able to see only his own point of view, and the deflated narcissist may be so acquiescent that he seems to have no view of his own at all, they are both rigidly locked into their positions and unable to shift flexibly. Through endless instances of analysis of transference enactments and of match, mismatch, and repair, through the action of the holding environment and the therapeutic object relationship (Grunes, 1984, 1998), and through the growth of mutual trust and mutual regulation, both patient and analyst eventually develop an increased respect and tolerance for each other. Ultimately they both learn or relearn that different people may view the same reality in different ways and that the patient's point of view and the analyst's point of view can both have reality and legitimacy. When this point is reached in the analysis, we then have two separate persons who treat each other as whole objects and who can negotiate between subjective and objective self-awareness. The achievement of this position is, to my mind, a prerequisite for the regular employment of classical interpretive techniques.

Of course, these days there is such an emphasis on mutuality, intersubjectivity, and the interpersonal that I have noticed a tendency to neglect those equally important moments, analogous to the gaze aversion of the child, when the patient withdraws from mutuality and creates a space of his own in which to process his own endogenous forces and enjoy his own volition and internal world. For integrating engagement and disengagement into a balanced view in both theory and practice is, in my experience, one of the most difficult things to do.

So far I have tried to present a brief overview of just a few of the many things we have learned about narcissism. Now some clinical illustrations that also point to issues I think we still do not quite understand.

You will remember the patient who had trouble with the narcissistic equilibrium between her subjective and objective awareness because she was either totally into herself and so excited that nothing else existed, or else she was her boyfriend's lover and then she could give him pleasure but not have any herself. Let me tell you about another woman, a very young 21-year-old who came to treatment because she was breaking up with her boyfriend. She had moved out of their apartment because she found that as long as she was living with her boyfriend she was unable to know whether she really wanted to stay with him or to leave him. She said, "It's only when I get away from Tom that I seem able to know what *I* want and not be influenced by what *he* wants. It seems that I may have to stay alone by myself for the rest of my life, because otherwise I become the slave of anyone who happens to come along and want something from me."

In fact, even after she broke off with the boyfriend he continued to come to her apartment at night and have sex with her because, as she reported, "If he wants it a lot, how can I say no? I can only refuse if I make a conscious effort to sort it out, to put my feelings before his, to listen, and to figure out what I really want for myself." In the language I have been using, she could either be totally into her own subjective awareness and therefore condemned to live alone forever, or else totally into her objective awareness of herself as her boyfriend's lover and therefore condemned to be his slave and unable to assert her true self.

Typically, of course, these lovers and spouses are displacements from the undifferentiated primal object; that is, these disruptions of awareness and object relations are traceable to disruptions of communication and differentiation that began in the early mother–infant dyad and continued as a cumulative trauma throughout childhood. In my experience, these patients respond very nicely to psychoanalysis but sometimes less easily to psychotherapy, because in many psychotherapies the appropriately deep, primitive transferences either cannot be achieved or else cannot be adequately managed.

Let me now add to this picture the case of a severely narcissistic young woman who could not form a relationship and had made several unsuccessful attempts at therapy. After some years of analysis she was able to marry and eventually to have a baby. However, unlike most of my patients who normally want to show me their new infants, she was adamant about not bringing her baby to treatment. It turned out she was afraid I would become too interested in the baby and thus deprive her of the one remaining place where she felt she was still getting attention. Clearly, the baby had not yet become part of her own narcissistic world in the way this generally happens during pregnancy and primary maternal preoccupation. Predictably, she had difficulty breast-feeding because, like my patient who had sexual problems with her boyfriend, this woman could either feed her baby without having pleasure herself, or else she could enjoy the sexual stimulation of breast-feeding but then she could not pay attention to the baby. The feeding had to be either for the baby or for herself, so she soon gave up trying and switched to the bottle. At this point in the analysis, her sense of self was still too fragile for mutuality to be a possibility, as was also evident in the transference, and it took quite some time before this disequilibrium began slowly to change.

Finally, let me mention a case where this change took place in quite a dramatic fashion. A number of years ago I was rash enough to undertake the analytic treatment of a woman who suffered from multiple personality disorder and severe mood swings. After several hectic years characterized by frightening enactments, desperate transference and countertransference crises, and repeated suicidal threats and gestures, one day she left this message on my answering machine:

> Dr. Bach, I just wanted to keep you informed that in addition to the many other things that psychoanalysis has deprived me of, I now seem to have lost the ability to commit suicide. I can never be positive that I had it, but I certainly scared myself a great number of times and was convinced that I was about to suicide. But yesterday I had probably the most painful day of my life, but I never seriously considered

suicide—that is, I never even for a moment flipped out or, as you call it, split off. I never seemed able to forget that I was the mother of little children and other things as well, and this was something that formerly didn't seem relevant to me and would never even have come into my mind.

Here we have a simple example of what I mean by interpenetration as the self-representations become suffused and permeated with important object representations and are raised to a higher level of integration so that what the patient referred to as "forgetting" that she was a mother was no longer possible. Of course, achieving this new level of self-integration was for her far from an unmixed blessing, and for a very long time thereafter she was furious at me for the many losses and deprivations that this process entailed.

Let me reiterate that what is at issue here is not just a simple shift from subjective to objective self-awareness, for even when suicidal she was always able, if reminded, to make this shift and objectively realize that she was, in fact, a mother. The problem was that this fact simply did not mean anything to her or was immediately forgotten until the expansion of her consciousness included her children in the sphere of her normal narcissistic omnipotence. Thus, what was required was not only a change in her ability to move between subjective and objective awareness but also in the organization of evocative constancy and her representational processes.

Meanwhile, for much of the time I was seeing her, this woman was either in states of hypomanic exaltation or in states of depression and excruciating psychic pain. This problem of the extraordinary pain suffered by many narcissistic patients has been more or less neglected in the literature. Although medication is occasionally of some help, it might also be useful to try to further our psychoanalytic understanding of this phenomenon.

Over the years, a number of clinicians have noted that many severely disturbed or narcissistic patients seem to have been born with lower thresholds and unusual sensitivities (Bergman and Escalona, 1949), making them more difficult to handle as infants and sometimes precipitating even in the early dyad a vicious cycle of mutual narcissistic injuries. More recently, Schore (1994) has drawn our attention to behavioral dysregulation in the dyad resulting in misregulation of the orbitofrontal cortex. As the mother mismatches her infant, sympathetic and parasympathetic arousal is abruptly switched on and off, leading to difficulties with smooth transitions and to a persistent dysregulation of the affective thermostat.

Since research in cognitive neurobiology (Teicher et al., 2003) has clearly demonstrated that the mother's language and emotional reactions psychobiologically influence the production of hormones and neurotransmitters in the child's brain, we know that the emotional interactions between mother and infant are imprinted into the developing nervous system. In this way, the mother's mind directly alters the child's body and nervous system, just as our own words and actions as psychoanalysts also influence the production of hormones and neurotransmitters in our patients' brains in ways similar to the psychoactive drugs, but sometimes with greater precision and fewer side effects.

But, returning to the problem of pain, I have alluded to both genetic and environmental factors and would like to emphasize the peculiarly psychoanalytic factor of *meaning*. In his clinical diary, Ferenczi (1932, p. 33) noted that, when seasick on a boat, if he synchronized his movements to those of the boat and surrendered himself to the larger unity of boat and sea and sky, his seasickness vanished. Comparing this experience to the traumatized child's efforts to escape into another world, he concluded that the context in which mental and physical events are experienced can dramatically alter the perception of those events. People with narcissistic disorders are similar to traumatized children, and one function of their narcissistic state is to keep them at a safe distance from the world that has caused them so much pain. When in treatment they are inevitably forced back into that world, they react as if they had stepped into a pot of boiling oil, with all the fury and the enactments that we know so well.

So pain management, both for patient and analyst, seems to be an integral part of this work. With the present state of our knowledge, it seems unfortunately necessary that the painful early dyadic interactions so ubiquitous in these patients be to some extent relived in the transference–countertransference and not simply aborted by distanced psychiatric management, premature interpretations, or the despair that the patient evokes in us.

For, indeed, in the depths of the transference–countertransference struggle that is conjured up with some of these patients, we are sometimes sorely tempted to abandon our own psychoanalytic attitude, if not to abandon the patient, or else to question our fundamental tenets or our own ability to help. Of course, the patient is trying to make us feel that there is no way out, for that is how he felt and feels, and, if we can metabolize these feelings and return them to him, there may yet be hope for both of us. And this is why I believe that, when we are working with these patients, the daily mental hygiene of cleaning up or clearing the countertransference is a crucial task and that it is mandatory, even for the most experienced analysts, to have a confidant, a peer group, or some other outlet where his feelings and doubts can be fully and frankly discussed.

When my patient experienced excruciating psychophysical pain during parts of her analysis as, to a lesser extent, I also did, she was in a primitive bad-mother transference to me that totally altered the meaning of her day-to-day existence. Like some voodoo doctor, it was I who was making her back hurt, her head explode, and her lungs gasp for breath. As month by month we slowly worked through these enactments, it was "as if a regressive experience is then brought into connection with an equivalent or corresponding one of higher mental complexity, [and] both of them gain in meaning" (Loewald, 1981, p. 29). Thus, in both the nursing and the therapeutic dyads, the links of action and feeling—through their interpenetration—become links of meaning. Loewald has noted how the various elements of action and feeling begin to encounter and know each other and become a context of meaning, which is one way of describing the organizing function of the ego. The linking is no longer one of repetitive action; it is one of representational connection.

That seems to be a good description of what happened to my patient and to me. One might also say that we had mutually regulated and enlarged each other's states of consciousness (Tronick, 1998) and that, in the process, my patient's fragmented phenomenal world and my own phenomenal world began to overlap in a larger and larger world that we both shared and could count on to be there for both of us, reliably, most of the time.

I have tried to suggest an overview of some important issues in narcissism, but I am embarrassingly aware of how much I have left out because of the inadequacies of my own understanding and because, ultimately, there is as yet so much we don't even realize that we do not know. When Freud (1914) first introduced narcissism to psychoanalysis, he wrote to Ferenczi, "Narcissism has arrived in

Berlin. . . . I am not satisfied with it" (Brabant et al., 1993, p. 546). Today, so many years later, we are all still working away at some of the very same issues that puzzled him then.

3

WORKING WITH THE
CHALLENGING PATIENT

Perhaps the primary problem when engaging the challenging patient is to build and retain what Ellman (1998) has called analytic trust. These challenging patients have generally lost their faith not only in their caregivers, spouses, and other objects, but also in the world itself as a place of expectable and manageable contingencies. Imagine what it would be like to inhabit a world where you never feel certain that your loved ones will be there when you come home, and not even certain that your home will still be there. Imagine what it is like to turn on your kitchen stove or start your car, always half-expecting them to explode. Imagine what it is like to feel that the air you breathe is toxic or that the oxygen supply is running out. These patients have lost their trust not only in people but also in the environment as a reliable place that will hold them safely. So one task we have is to restore this faith and to rebuild it again and again as it inevitably gets lost in the vicissitudes of the transference.

We do this by making the analytic consulting room a safe and reliable space and by being absolutely truthful with the patient about everything that occurs in this space and that happens between us. Whenever the situation becomes momentarily unreliable, sometimes because we have failed—as we inevitably must over the years—we recognize this and analyze our own reactions as well as the patient's, for there is no way that a patient who mistrusts everything will trust us at all if we insist on leaving ourselves out of the equation. There is a way of being absolutely straight with the patient without indulging in confessions, apologia, or gross parameters, and this way is different for everyone and must be worked out differently with each individual patient.

I say worked out with the patient because, even if the patient is unable to engage in mutual collaboration, and at first most of these patients are not, *we* are always collaborating with them by going along with their vision of reality even when they reject ours. In the transference regression these patients do not really experience themselves as completely separate, and so they cannot believe in or coexist with separate psychic realities. The idea that the same reality can be viewed in different ways by different people, and that the patient's *and* the analyst's views can both have truth and legitimacy, is often beyond their emotional comprehension. Thus a true collaboration between two independent persons may be impossible, and we must defer to the patient's vision of reality until he becomes able to tolerate our presence and psychic reality in the room with him.

By this means we enter the patient's phenomenal world and begin to build analytic trust, which at first may be a trust in the security of the analytic setup more than in us as a person. For in many cases we do not really exist as an object until we make a mistake, or until something happens to make us loom up as a threatening stranger. Such disruptions of the budding narcissistic transference and therapeutic alliance may result from the patient's impulses or our own ineptness, and may be expressed in a mutual enactment or a projective identification, but these disruptions demand immediate understanding and rectification.

Each episode of attempted alliance, its disruption, and the repair of the alliance raises the mutual trust to a higher level—we have gone through something together and survived it. Each episode of mismatch, disruption, and repair is also an ongoing process of regulation of the dyadic system. I am emphasizing the simultaneous emergence and interplay of mutual trust and mutual regulation in the analytic dyad. But what do I mean by mutual regulation?

In the days when psychologists often experimented with conditioning rats, a well-known cartoon showed one rat in a cage telling another, "I've got this guy trained by now—every time I press the lever, he gives me a pellet of food!" The psychologist, of course, felt that he was conditioning or regulating the rat, but, indeed, they had arrived at a jointly satisfactory state of mutual regulation. They could trust each other to be consistent, reliable, mutually satisfying objects. Now this sort of mutual regulation is continually occurring, often without awareness, in the successful mother–infant dyad and also in the successful patient–analyst dyad (Beebe and Lachmann, 2005). The analytic dyad is distinguished by the analyst's insistence that difficulties in the relation should ultimately be verbalized and analyzed, not just remediated or glossed over. But since so many of our challenging patients are products of poorly regulated mother–infant dyads or badly regulated family systems, it is not always easy to know how to handle any particular situation in its immediacy.

Let me be doubly concrete and imagine a situation where a patient complains of being too hot or too cold in the consulting room and asks that the temperature be changed. Do we simply comply as social convention demands? Or do we question and investigate further or, having checked that the temperature is normal, do we make an interpretation about possible emotional reactions and physiological changes? I suspect there is no recipe for answering these kinds of questions and that the complexities of mutual regulation in the treatment process can be addressed only through the complexities of mutual discussion in the supervision process in which the two parties have learned to trust each other and to speak openly. In this sense, good supervision is similar to good therapy.

I hope that by now I have made it clear why I feel that analytic trust is based on and grows with successful mutual regulation. The patient arrives to find the analyst always there and usually on time; his own irregularities of arrival, of thought, and of emotion are met with temperance and understanding; the couch is always there, the temperature is usually comfortable, and nothing physical ever explodes. Slowly, he begins to develop trust, first in the physical regularities of the analytic holding world, then in the

process by which each mismatch is slowly understood and repaired, then in the reliability of the analyst as some kind of part-object or selfobject, and, ultimately, in the reliability of the analyst as
a separate whole object.

Meanwhile, we are uncovering and analyzing those regulatory
challenges that most of these patients have, even if they are unaware of them. I am talking about disturbances of breathing, of
sleeping, of eating, of bodily functioning and orientation in the
world, but I also include disturbances of emotional regulation that
are inseparable from the physiological; for example, dysregulation
of affect so that highs and lows are too extreme, too prolonged, or
too rapidly cycled and unpredictable. Above all, I want to draw your
attention to a kind of intermittent decathexis of the object (Furman
and Furman, 1984) so that object constancy is almost always in
question. Many of these patients have experienced this intermittent
decathexis from their own caregivers, who attended to them only
when they were needed as narcissistic objects. As adults, the patients tend not only to repeat this intermittent decathexis with their
own objects but also to experience themselves as only intermittently
alive and coherent—their own self-constancy is always in question.
Of course, regulatory problems like disturbances in orientation,
emotional regulation, or intermittent decathexis will emerge in the
transference anyhow, with the patient either producing it in you or
getting you to produce it in him. But since these transference reactions are so often accompanied by intense rage and other blinding
emotions, I think the analyst is at a great advantage if the subject
has already been raised and discussed in its historical context.

We are talking about people who, because of an early or cumulative trauma or because of an early failure of the environment to
fit in with their temperaments or endowments, have lost or never
even developed a trust in the regularities of their physical environment, let alone their object environment. These early disturbances
of mutual regulation, which, as Schore (1994) has demonstrated,
get built into the developing nervous system, lead inevitably to
dysregulation of the drive economy and to disturbances of object
relations.

Although the earliest nonverbal and verbal interactions can profoundly influence brain chemistry and synaptic growth, I believe
that later verbal interactions and mutual regulation can also influence brain chemistry and can alter behavior at least as much as

psychotropic medications. At the beginning, the infant responds to the mother–infant interaction at the sensorimotor level and over the next few years learns to respond at the symbolic level as well. But even adults, particularly challenging patients, continue to respond at the sensorimotor-physiological level since that is where their earliest mutual regulations went awry. These sensorimotor-physiological responses frequently manifest in inappropriate or negative transference reactions or enactments, which are often as difficult for the patient to understand as they are for the analyst. I try in the first sessions with these patients to get both an overview of the dynamic picture and a history of the early dysregulation with which it is so often entwined. This narrative frequently interests the patient sufficiently to try to fill in the missing data or to verify it on his own initiative. I find that working in this way from the very beginning is a great help in dealing with transference disruptions, in understanding and managing them, and in arriving at the better regulated interaction that is the foundation of basic trust.

Naturally, I go along with those patients who refuse to talk about anything but the immediate here and now, but I view it as a kind of defensive distortion. Normally, past, present, and future interconnect and continuously retranscribe each other, so that touching a life at any point should connect us with the whole. But since challenging patients are so frequently disconnected from their past and from vital dimensions of themselves, it is easier to move the therapy if one can find a handle on both the past and the present.

Here let me simply state my belief that controversies between opposing standpoints such as "here and now" versus "then and there," deficit versus conflict, hermeneutics versus science, interpretation versus holding, and other similar oppositions and shibboleths often represent false dichotomies that promote or impose a type of political correctness that keeps us from thinking and speaking about what we actually do. I recall that in the not-too-distant past the fear of employing "parameters" made a whole generation of analysts talk and act as if the technique police were just around the corner. So, in the range of positions about the analyst's stance with the patient, it still seems to me that the best place to be most of the time is as close to the patient's experiential world as possible.

Just to put a little flesh on these bones, let me give a brief example from a consultation I recently did:

A competent and experienced analyst presents a young professional woman, attractive and successful, whom he has seen in therapy for three months and who is threatening to quit. The patient complains of her need to attach herself to some man, but when he gets too close she feels obliged to break it off. She divorced her husband after starting an affair with an older man who lived in another country. When this older man phoned her to break off the relationship, she developed frightening somatic symptoms, called the Emergency Medical Service, and threw herself into the arms of the responding ambulance driver, who was obliged to hold her and caress her to calm her down. She then had a brief affair with this driver that helped carry her through the period of breakup with the older man. She is able to say that her mother was always nervous and agitated, that the beloved older man was, in her own words, a "fantasy father figure," and that her father used to rub her legs to put her to sleep, but none of this material seems to help her or to engage her.

When the therapist takes a long weekend vacation, she goes to a psychic, who gives her a piece of stone that makes her feel more calm and secure. Over the weekend she joins a group of Buddhists who meditate and chant. When the therapist tries to connect these enactments with his absence, she appears disdainful and seems to find his suggestions vaguely amusing. Shortly thereafter she complains that therapy is boring and is not helping, and she makes plans to leave. The therapist repeatedly focuses on her need to attach herself to some man and to break things off when the man gets too close. When this interpretation does not seem to help, the therapist comes for a consultation.

Talking over all this with the therapist in the way I have done here helps him find a way into the case. He remembers the patient telling him that, when she first went to kindergarten, her mother dropped her off in front of the schoolhouse, and the patient became disoriented and never found her way to the classroom. He remembers that the patient always envied those little girls whose mothers shampooed their hair, because her mother never touched her like that. As the therapist begins to inquire into other areas of self- and mutual regulation, the patient becomes more responsive.

As a young woman she felt that she lacked "discipline," and she moved to Germany in the hope that living in Germany might instill some discipline in her. Now he helps her understand that her "lack of discipline" is really an inability to self-regulate, which is connected to her mother's failures to help her regulate when the patient was a child. She stops talking about leaving and becomes more interested in her history. The treatment is under way.

I have been emphasizing mutual regulatory processes both because they are terribly important for more disturbed patients and also because until recently we did not hear much about them in Freudian theory, in which the economic point of view had gone out of fashion. Nevertheless, many of these patients know there is something wrong with their regulatory processes, but they are unable to conceptualize what it is and have given themselves such explanations as "I don't have any discipline," "My trouble is I love too much," "I'm disorganized and disoriented, and it's genetic," and the like. They are often interested in discovering that these lifelong issues may stem from a chronic dysregulation of the early dyad or family system and that self-regulation can be learned.

Approaching these issues from the economic or regulatory side is usually much easier for challenging patients, most of whom have problems with reflective self-awareness and symbolization. The patient who went to see a psychic while her analyst was away could not see any connection between these two events and would probably have been frightened and fled if she had. But I do believe that talking with her about the stone the psychic gave her and about her psychophysiological reactions to its solidity and permanence would have elicited her own feelings of tenuousness and *impermanence,* which underlay her belief that she lacked discipline. I would then anticipate associations about childhood attempts at self-healing by playing with solid objects or putting herself in situations, like the Buddhist chanting, that gave her a temporary sense of solidity and stability. If she became interested in this possibility, we might then track the changes in her feelings of insubstantiality, and she might, only after a very long time, begin to relate these to the analyst's physical or emotional absence.

Even in this oversimplified case vignette, there are so many things going on simultaneously and so many possible theoretical levels and viewpoints that we may well wonder how to sort them out or where to begin. Do we address the patient's complaint that she needs to attach herself to some man but then feels compelled to break it off? The therapist did try to make just such transference interpretations when the patient threatened to leave the analysis, but to no avail. Should we address her affair with the oedipal older man, who calmed her and soothed her as her own father had when he used to rub her legs to put her to sleep? She makes these connections herself, because she knows about the Oedipus complex, but they touch nothing in her. Should we deal with her anger at her mother, who abandoned her on her first day at school and presumably never shampooed her lovingly as she imagined other mothers doing? Should we interpret her father's foot massages as substitutes for her mother's shampoos? While all these dynamic connections are valid enough, I am reasonably sure that making them initially would have gotten nowhere.

If we are able to listen carefully and with enough attention, patients will usually *prescribe* exactly what is necessary for their healing to begin. In this case, in response to a long weekend break, the patient reacts by finding a hard, permanent, massageable object and a state of consciousness in which she can feel alone when surrounded by others. We know, then, that she is unusually sensitive to separations but is able to deal with them only in a concrete way. She requires a regulatory dyad that will stabilize and solidify both her self-regulation and her analytic trust, yet at the same time she is likely to struggle against those very parameters, such as increased frequency of sessions and use of the couch, that would help the dyad become regulatory. We handle this dilemma by remaining phenomenologically close to her concrete use of objects and things in the interests of self-regulation, while at the same time trying to relate them to the dysregulation in her earlier history.

Thus, with these challenging patients, we start from the concrete and move to the abstract. We start from the physical and move to the mental and emotional, just as we always start from whatever is self-centered and only gradually move to whatever is object centered. We do this because the deficiencies in their symbolization and self-awareness lead them to communicate impulsively by enactments that are sometimes unintelligible and often uninterpretable. Challenging patients respond at this behavioral and sensorimotor level because their basic mistrust and ongoing dysregulation have prevented them from developing the kind of separateness and potential space, the impulse control, the symbolic abilities, and the degree of self-reflection that are pre-requisites for the use of classical analytic technique.

One might say that classical technique assumes a large degree of shared reality between analyst and patient, an assumption that usually does not hold true with challenging patients. One way that children learn about reality is by learning to read their mother's face and learning that she has a mind and feelings that are some-times in accord with theirs and sometimes different. Ideally, they learn that their own feelings and their mother's feelings both have reality and legitimacy. But when challenging patients say, "I never knew what my mother was thinking or feeling," they frequently also mean that they still cannot read how other people think or feel and that they still cannot believe that their own feelings are real or legitimate.

Caregivers affirm reality by legitimizing the child's emotions and thoughts. If the mother's face conveys one meaning and her metacommunication in other modalities generally conveys a con-tradictory meaning, then the child may not become schizophrenic but is likely to be a challenging patient. Problems of reality are tre-mendously amplified in the psychoanalytic situation because of the potential conflict between the psychic realities of patient and analyst and because of the many different levels of reality on which the treatment exists. Do the patient and analyst "really" love each other or "really" want to kill each other, or are their feelings only metaphoric? At times they certainly feel real enough to both partic-ipants. We hope that the analyst can move freely between levels of reality and encompass the metaphor, but the challenging patient who could never read his mother's face and has never been sure of his reality has great difficulty achieving this equilibrium.

In the psychoanalytic situation, this conflict often emerges as an underlying sadomasochistic struggle over whose version of re-ality should be accepted. Freud (1915a) spoke of "women of ele-mental passionateness" who treat transference love as real love and "refuse to accept the *psychical* in place of the material" (pp. 166–167). But one cannot interpret the transference, which is partly a metaphor, to a patient whose mental organization is un-able to accommodate the symbolism of metaphor. In practice, such patients will confuse or confabulate what should be transferential and symbolic issues with *real* issues of love or death, and will strug-gle with the analyst as if he were *in fact* refusing to love them or even trying to rape or kill them. The patient I discussed had a very real fear of her own "elemental passionateness," which was one reason she was so reluctant to allow herself to become deeply involved in treatment.

These patients are unable to understand that *different people can view the same reality in different ways and that their point of view and the analyst's point of view can both have reality and legitimacy*. They have great difficulty in shifting between levels of meaning, symbolism, and reality, and it is precisely at these transitions or shifts between levels, contexts, and frameworks that most transference disruptions occur—but also that the greatest potential for change exists (Bach, 1994).

The patient, who in response to a weekend break, went to a psychic and got a stone to calm her, would very likely have become angry and upset had the analyst continued to insist on the connection between these two events. I believe that to conceptualize this occurrence as denial is misleading. The patient would have experienced the analyst's interpretations and insistence just as she experienced her mother's dropping her off outside the schoolhouse—as a dysregulation and an emotional desertion. She would have become confused and disoriented and felt lost. This confusion, which is a *psychic disorientation* at transitions between levels of symbolism and contextual frameworks, may often be paralleled by or experienced as a *physical disorientation* at transitions between places and events.

In treatment we hold the patient in the analytic framework, and a good deal of our effort goes toward maintaining and adjusting that framework, which the patient is constantly probing to test the levels of reality and to learn how much he can trust us. Through enactments and counterenactments, through projective identifications that are contained and metabolized, through constructions and interpretations, and through the vicissitudes of the transference, a transitional space develops in which confusion, ambiguity, and separation can be tolerated and explored. This feels to the patient very much as if, instead of her mother's dropping her off outside the school, the analyst has instead taken her by the hand and accompanied her into the classroom.

Eventually, a psychoanalytic space evolves that can contain two whole, autonomous individuals who are capable of loving and hating each other and of trying to deal with each other's psychic realities. By then, the patient's language and symbolizing capacity will also be linked to his real affects and sensorimotor behavior, and the analyst's interpretations will be heard not as boundary violations or contradictory communications, but as potentially helpful contributions. But by then, of course, the treatment is almost over.

Many of these modifications of technique that analysts have advanced over the years originated with classical technique and have a historical continuity with it. They were introduced as it became clear to some that classical technique did not always work well for patients with severe problems of trust, self-regulation, self-reflexivity, and symbolization. The classical method, when strictly enforced with these patients, sometimes resulted in losing a patient completely or producing a stalemate or a pseudoanalysis, in which the patient goes through the motions of an analysis out of compliance or desperation, but without belief.

Some of these modifications include:

1. Holding or containing, including pacification, soothing, and emotional regulation through interpenetration of affects.
2. Accepting projections of all kinds and returning them in a usably metabolized form.
3. Reintegrating, synthesizing, and sustaining a sense of continuity. This includes maintaining a holistic rather than a partial or fragmentary view of the patient.
4. Framing and discussing spatiotemporal and bodily parameters.
5. Lending oneself to, living with, and only eventually interpreting enactments.
6. Verbal and bodily expressions of empathy and affective attunement.
7. The ability to survive the patient's transferential onslaughts while still retaining some analytic capacity.

The consistent use of these functions should help the patient feel that he is present and alive in some important way in the analyst's mind, and also help the analyst keep the patient alive in a continuous way in his own mind. Reciprocally, the patient will be learning to keep the analyst consistently alive and useful in his own mind, and the analyst will also begin to feel that he lives in the mind of his patient.

Working from the technical stance I have described, I find that challenging patients often may and sometimes may not become amenable to classical technique. But at least they always know that the transference feelings they experienced in the treatment felt real to them and were acknowledged by me, and that the unconscious fantasies that emerged belonged to them and not to me. For people who already have difficulty moving between levels of reality, nothing can be more important than *learning to trust their own feelings* in the heat of the analytic situation. If they can also learn to accept my feelings and my differences, then they have come a very long way toward resolving the sadomasochistic struggle over whose version of reality can be trusted. And the primacy of this struggle, between awareness and defense, between self and other, and between love and hate is, after all, an essential part of what I understand as the psychoanalytic vision of life.

4

A MIND OF ONE'S OWN

Then felt I like some watcher of the skies
When a new planet swims into his ken
Or like stout Cortez when with eagle eyes
He star'd at the Pacific—and all his men
Look'd at each other with a wild surmise—
Silent, upon a peak in Darien.
                    —John Keats, "On First Looking
                         into Chapman's Homer"

I believe that we in the Western world find ourselves in the midst of a change of viewpoint that will become increasingly important in this second millennium and that is bound to affect us in every field of endeavor. For almost 100 years now, we have slowly been coming to understand that an object we are observing, whether an atom, a virus, or a patient, is not totally independent from the person doing the observing and the means employed to make that observation. In our own field this has led to a profusion and confusion of theories about intersubjectivity and transference–countertransference that will take decades to think through, understand, and sort out. Just to give one simple example: while 30 years ago I might have ventured a strong opinion when asked to evaluate the analyzability of a patient, today I find this question more difficult to answer without also taking into account who the proposed analyst might be, that is, the total system including both what the analysand brings to the encounter and also what the analyst brings.

In physics this has led to a similar imbroglio, typified by the impassioned debate between Einstein and Bohr (1963), which has produced theories about other worlds and nonlocal action that seem to surpass in fantasticality both science-fiction and the fantasies of even our most psychotic patients. The field of medicine is undergoing a corresponding evolution: our understanding of disease is giving way to a larger field view wherein the host and the host's immune functions and mental attitudes become as relevant as the attacking virus or bacteria. Since allopathic medicine and the germ theory have contributed to extraordinary advances in medical care over the past century, the medical establishment is inclined to emphasize these past successes while ignoring those chronic health problems, including mental health problems, which are less susceptible to representation and treatment with this approach. The practical consequence has been the rapid expansion of alternative medicine so that Americans apparently now spend more money on alternative medical services than on allopathic medicine.

Likewise in the humanities and social sciences, this evolutionary change in our thinking has led, for example, in literature, to deconstructive readings that question whether the author is really the authority on the meaning of his text and that may go so far as to claim that a text has no inherent meaning whatsoever but is simply the container for whatever meanings a particular reader or society may ascribe to it.

As we try to grasp the far-reaching implications of these changes both for our field and for others, we sense that there are at least two opposing visions of the world, proponents of each having staked their claim to absolute truth at the expense of the other. On one hand, there are those who emphasize subjectivity, relativism, contingency, and the deconstructive approach and who view all situations as mutual coconstructions of the involved participants. To return to my example about analyzability, such people might feel that nothing at all can be said about a patient's analyzability unless we know who the analyst is and what the parameters of the analytic situation are.

On the other hand, there are those who lay claim to realistic, empirical, objective, and so-called scientific observations and who, in the extreme, might claim that any patient can be equally well analyzed by any well-trained analyst regardless of the degree of fit, the social context, or the analyst's personal peculiarities. While there are many gradations between these two extremes, for convenience I call the first group, who believe in the mutual coconstruction of reality, the "constructionists," and the second group, who believe in the absolute existence of an independent reality, the "essentialists." In certain ways this controversy historically resembles the nature–nurture controversy, with the constructionists emphasizing nurture and the essentialists emphasizing nature.

At the risk of caricaturing these extreme positions, which not everyone holds, let me remind you of some of the heated debates they have engendered in our own field. Constructionists, for example, because they believe in cocreation, are likely to feel that analyzability is primarily a function of the dyad, that mutual enactments and self-disclosures are inevitable and even desirable, that socially instilled values, developmental deficits, and implicit behaviors are fundamental, and that holding, mirroring, and moments of meeting are the primary engines of psychotherapeutic change. Essentialists, on the other hand, feel that one can say a great deal about analyzability apart from the therapist because the pathology is structurally intrinsic and defines the patient independently of the context. They tend to believe that enactments should be interpreted and self-disclosure avoided, that endogenous drives and conflicts take precedence over deficits, and that the primary or even the sole engine of psychotherapeutic change is verbal interpretation, and especially transference interpretation.

Like many others, I find myself at neither of these extremes. I do believe that probably most of these issues will eventually sort themselves out with the adoption of a larger point of view that may synthesize both positions and incorporate ways of thinking about thinking that are more sophisticated than we are able today even to imagine.

Patients, whose conflicts often resemble those of philosophers, can also be either constructionists or essentialists. That is, they can feel that their thinking and sense of self are completely field dependent and relative to the people and context they find themselves in, or they can feel that their thinking and sense of self are completely field independent, an essential truth that depends not on context or other people but on some self-determined or inborn sense of identity and reality. Bearing all this in mind, I want to show you how these issues affect our clinical work by going over some experiences I have had in the past several years working with patients who complain that they have difficulties with thinking.

In the past, of course, difficulties in thinking were classified as thought disorders and were taken to be one of the primary symptoms of the schizophrenias or psychoses. Later on, under the influence of David Rapaport (1951) and the psychological testing movement (Rapaport, Gill, and Schafer, 1945, 1946), it became clear that every personality category implied a specific and idiosyncratic way of thinking. Thus one might categorize a hysterical thinking disorder, an obsessive thinking disorder, or even a narcissistic thinking disorder, about which I have frequently written over the years (Bach, 1977, 1994). Indeed, diagnostic psychological testing is based on the assumption that a psychologist, using tests, will be able to detect and specify the particular kind of thinking disorder that is characteristic of each diagnostic syndrome.

But in the changed intellectual climate of this second millennium, we have come to understand in a deeper way not only that the observer and the observed are part of one system but that the mind and the body are also one. Any thinking disorder is also a disorder of the chemical environment and the synaptic architecture of the brain; that is, a thinking disorder is, by definition, also a brain disorder, and vice versa.

Similarly, whether the patient complains of a disorder in thinking, such as obsessive thoughts, or a disorder of emotions, such as self-esteem fluctuations or mood irregularities, or even a disorder of bodily functioning, such as the irregular breathing of panic attacks or paresthesias or a paralyzed limb, he is complaining of a disorder in self-regulation of body or mind or feelings. We understand that to influence the one is to influence all the others because they are, in effect, different manifestations of one and the same system.

Thus, thinking and brain disorders may be initiated by such apparently endogenous internal factors or events as genetic endowment, or the hormonal surges of adolescence, or menopause, or a stroke, or by such apparently exogenous environmental factors or events as negligent parenting, traumatic shocks, or even a sharp decline in the stock market. Fortunately, there is now considerable evidence that the chemical and structural changes of a brain disorder, which may sometimes be reversed or modified by the direct intervention of neurosurgery or psychopharmacology, can sometimes also be reversed or modified by certain kinds of talking and social contact; that is, psychotherapy can change brain chemistry and brain architecture just as psychopharmacology and psychosurgery can, but perhaps in different ways and sometimes with fewer negative side effects.

I am maintaining that thoughts, emotions, and the body that contains them are all different aspects of an interrelated system. A parent who consistently responds to his infant child with a frozen face every time she smiles at him may eventually induce in her not only a problematic emotional development but also a problematic cognitive development and a problematic neurological development. To the extent that these developments are reversible, they may be changed either through early intervention in the dyad by teaching the parent to respond more appropriately or later through psychotherapy, psychopharmacology, or perhaps yet unimagined interventions, though each modality may produce different kinds of changes.

What I want to discuss here are some general principles involved in reversing or modifying such an early induced thought, brain, body, and emotional disorder in adults. While this may seem like a tall order when conceptualized in this way, it is really nothing more than what some therapists have been doing all along, similar to the position Molière's (1670) bourgeois gentleman found himself in when he was amazed to discover that he had been talking prose all his life.

Let me descend from the heights of theory with a simple clinical example.

A patient of mine, Bob, once casually mentioned that as an adolescent whenever he borrowed the family car his father insisted that he never move the seat adjustment. Since the father at that time was a good head taller than Bob, Bob had learned to drive while barely able to see over the hood of the car and he continued to drive like that for many years. Clearly, this story is emblematic of the many ways in which Bob's father could not really allow his son to be in the "driver's seat" or to be different from himself in thought, feeling, or even bodily configuration, and this zero tolerance for differences led to distortions of Bob's own life in all these areas. In fact, it was not until Bob was in analysis and his wife remarked on his peculiar way of driving that this distortion became conscious and Bob was finally able to adjust his seat to fit his own bodily dimensions. Bob's being scrunched down in the driver's seat was also a model for how he was scrunched down in both his emotional life and in his thinking. Most of these constraints had been completely out of Bob's awareness before he came into analysis and yet constructive forces were also unconsciously at work trying to undo their effects.

It turned out that for a long time Bob had been a devotee of a particular form of yoga that emphasized unrestricted breathing and stretching, and he had become quite expert at it. I took this interest in yoga to be an unconscious attempt on the part of his body–mind to counteract the constrictions of the scrunched-down position his father had imposed on him and to which he had conformed himself in one way but struggled against in another. From Bob's point of view, he had learned to drive in the same way he had learned so many other things—by going along with the family system. An outside observer might have thought that he seemed strangely compliant to an unusual demand, but it might have taken a psychoanalyst to note the life-affirming rebellion inherent in his practice of yoga. This is a simple example of an observation that has often amazed me—that the mind and body work together in attempts to regulate the self-system and that the analyst can note these efforts and encourage them without violating parameters if he can only find a broader perspective from which to view the patient's dilemma.

Finding a broader perspective is, of course, not easy, particularly since so many different schools of analysis proclaim that their own perspective is the only truth. Experience suggests that what patients talk about is highly correlated with what they think interests their analysts—Freudian patients feel they should talk about sex and aggression, Jungian patients feel they should talk about symbolism and religion, and Kleinian patients see their projections and reparations as the essentials of psychic life. Meanwhile, some of the research (Orlinsky and Geller, 1993) suggests that a major factor for therapeutic success is the warmth and availability of the therapist and the congruent personalities of the therapeutic couple, regardless of the theories the therapist or patient might hold. Other research (Freedman et al., 1999) insists on the importance of frequency and continuity, as well as on the ability of the therapy to promote self-observation. Of course, these apparent disparities make more sense from a systems perspective, and to me they make particular sense if we view the therapeutic dyad as a reworking of the original dyad in which the continuing goal of each participant was to understand how the mind and the body of the other person really worked.

From one perspective, good parenting as well as good therapy entails a lively interest in how one's own mind and body work, *both separate from and in conjunction with the mind and body of another person,* and often the fewer preconceptions that we bring to the task, the better. Both parenting and therapy are good examples of on-the-job learning, where some preparation may be helpful but can never substitute for the real thing. So mother and baby, when facing each other for the first time, are both novices in their particular dyad, and, indeed, the infant, unencumbered by theory, is often a much faster learner than the mother.

We know that the mother is trying to find out how the baby works—how and when it wants to eat, sleep, and eliminate and what it thinks and feels about her ministrations. And the baby is also trying to find out the complementary information about the mother and somehow to balance out this information about what the mother wants with its own, often uncontrollable, urges of hunger, fatigue, and the other endogenous forces that drive it on. The mother too is struggling with her own endogenous forces: her fatigue, her shifting hormones, perhaps also her resentment against her husband or against a hated sibling with whom she might identify the baby. Thus, from the beginning, the learning situation is disturbed by dark unconscious and preconscious forces that both participants bring to the drama and that complicate it immensely.

You remember Bob, whose scrunched-down position driving his father's car was emblematic of the distortions the field had induced in both his mental and his bodily functioning. It turned out that Bob's acquiescence to the Procrustean bed his father had laid for him meant even more than surrender to his oedipal fear or guilt. Until a point about a year into analysis, I had formed only a vague picture of Bob's mother until one day, when complaining about his confusion and difficulties in thinking at work, he casually mentioned that as a child he could never find the forks for dinner. I asked,

T: What do you mean, never find the forks?
B: Oh, you know, there wouldn't be any forks, and I would ask Mom where they were and she would say, "Go look in the drawer."
T: And so . . .
B: Well, the drawers would be all messed up and I couldn't find the forks.
T: How do you mean, all messed up?
B: You know, old rubber bands and paper clips and recipes and all kinds of stuff you had to look through to find the forks.
T: You mean the silverware wasn't organized in some kind of way?
B: No, everything was just thrown in the drawer. . . . I was surprised when my wife insisted on buying a special holder to put the silverware in. That was the first time I had ever seen such a thing.

By now, of course, it had dawned on me that we were somehow talking about the internal organization of Bob's mother's mind and, by extension, of his own mind, and about his own confusion and difficulties with thinking. It would take many months before this became clear to Bob and many years of work before he could reconfigure his own mind to make things more logical and easily accessible.

Of course, not every caretaker whose child complains of a thinking difficulty is disorganized in the same way as Bob's mother was. Others may appear organized in some ways and chaotic in others, and a pattern of erratic or intermittent inattention or disorganization is quite common. But in Bob's case his mother's difficulty separating her silverware was emblematic of her difficulties with separation in general: with mentally separating from anyone, with taking distance on her own opinions, and with seeing her own child as a separate entity.

Children who are not seen as separate entities remain enmeshed in the early dyadic state of consciousness; they have difficulty seeing themselves or others as separate and at the deepest level *they do not feel entitled to have a life or a mind of their own*. Even when these children are able to *physically* separate they often continue to feel guilty about it, and they find mental separation especially frightening to achieve.

Whatever the particular state of maternal or familial organization or disorganization, if the child cannot separate himself from it, he will be unable to gain any perspective on it. Thus the mother's mental processes and often the family processes remain impenetrable to the child who feels in a continual state of confusion (cf. Fonagy et al., 2002). If Bob's mother had been able to say, "I know the drawer's messy, but I'm sure the forks are there somewhere," it might have made all the difference, because this would have meant that she was able to take some perspective on her own behavior and she might then have allowed him some room for his own perspective.

But she was unable to view herself reflectively and therefore was unable to allow Bob to see her objectively or to see himself reflectively. Children like this cannot figure out how their caregiver's mind works and consequently cannot understand how their own mind works or, eventually, the minds of other people or the mind of the analyst in the transference. Patients whose minds have not been legitimized by their parents feel confused and frantic. One of them, speaking of his mother, said, "She is this dark, brooding, amorphous cloud of secrets. Is she selfish, or is she scared? Does she love my father, or does she hate him? You just can't tell. . . . She'll drive you crazy. . . . I don't want to think about her. . . . If I think about her, then I can't think."

Many of these patients remain, throughout their lives, consciously or unconsciously obsessed in a very concrete, literal way with questions of epistemology: Do other minds exist? How can you know the mind of another person? Can I trust a person to reveal his mind? How can I tell if he's lying? Am I dealing with a human mind or just a computer simulating a mind? Is my mind human? Am I really alive? Does death really exist? And so forth. These patients live in a constant state of ontological insecurity, which they experienced as infants and which is revived again in the analytic transference.

This, then, was Bob's dilemma, and it is characteristic of people with thinking disorders. The patient is confused and anxious about having a mind of his own that exists independent of other people's minds. Sometimes this confusion pervades all areas of life and sometimes only selected areas, depending on the caregiver's specific deficiencies and prohibitions. Sometimes the patient does not know what he is feeling and does not even know how to think about what he is feeling. Often he cannot describe anything about himself or his family except the facts, so that the therapist does not get a real feeling for the people involved. Being factual about relationships may give the appearance of objectivity, but it may also indicate a repression of the emotional context of events and, often, an actual deficiency in relationships with people and even with things.

I recently came across an excellent description of this deficiency in the autobiography of the distinguished British literary critic Sir Frank Kermode (1999), whose title, interestingly enough, is *Not Entitled*. Here he describes how, as a child, he was so totally inadequate in interpersonal as well as motor skills that his teachers all believed he was purposely trying to make fun of them and repeatedly punished him for his behavior. Let me quote:

> Since nobody any longer can compel me to carve or draw, or even hang a picture straight, it may be supposed that my incapacity became a trifling problem once the pains of childhood humiliation had faded. But it has persisted, and may be related to some of my difficulties in dealing with other people, especially women. I lack what appears to be in others a perfectly ordinary skill or tact in handling not only things but also persons. I notice this ability among children in playgrounds and people in pubs; or when somebody draws a sketch map, peels an orange, assumes an attitude obviously correct but not in my repertoire, or embarks on a seduction. They all seem to know what it takes; [but] where and how they found it out is a mystery to me. My lack of *qualities so natural to others that they never needed even to congratulate themselves on having them* was emphasized by my being a fat boy [p. 54].

Psychoanalysts have often noted Kermode's complaint of deficiency in "what appears to be in others a perfectly ordinary skill or tact in handling not only things but persons." John Gedo (1984) has for years described it as a deficiency in a learned skill, and infant researchers and I have often referred to it as a deficit of self-

and mutual regulation or as a defect in narcissistic equilibrium or procedural knowledge. This has most recently been given extensive attention by the infant researchers in the Boston Change Process Study Group (Stern, 1998), who label this ability "implicit relational knowing" and connect it with the ongoing preverbal proceedings between mother and infant. Kermode (1999), who is an intellectual, does not complain of difficulties with thinking, but he does remark that the deficiency of skills he describes is profoundly implicated in his rather tenuous relations with both people and things.

It is worth noting that patients who complain of confusion or difficulties with thinking also often have difficulties with implicit relational knowing and vice versa, if only because one cannot feel awkward or lacking implicit knowledge in the presence of someone and not have this affect the way one listens, understands, and speaks with them. The Stern (1998) group suggests that there are two modes of therapeutic action: verbal interpretations acting in the domain of *explicit* knowledge, which can alter conscious or unconscious processes, and what they call relational or behavioral "moments of meeting," in which the *"implicit* knowledge of each partner gets altered by creating a new and different intersubjective context between them—the relationship has changed." They believe that "this process requires no interpretation and need not be made verbally explicit" (p. 302).

But I suggest that these two domains interpenetrate and are not really separate, or, if they indeed seem separate, that is a pathological outcome that needs to be understood. For the baby is interested in finding out how his own mind and body works *both in relation to and independently of the mind and body of his caregiver,* and the distinctions that we make later between explicit and implicit, conscious and unconscious, verbal and nonverbal, and one-person and two-person are meaningless to the baby.

Of course, one very important aspect of combining *explicit* representational thinking with *implicit* relational knowing is that this is a fuller way of acknowledging another person's mind. But under good-enough circumstances the child develops both a mind of his own and the ability to accept the mind of another person without surrendering his own mind. And that is why those of us who as children were lucky enough to have been adequately parented can enjoy ontological security as adults without being constantly persecuted by worries about whether we or other people do really exist, are only pretending, or can really be relied on.

For the ontological security that leads to a basic trust in life and trust in the analytic situation (Erikson, 1956; Ellman, 1998) is most often disturbed by splitting in the areas that I have described: splits between mind and body, between implicit and explicit knowledge, between intersubjective and intrasubjective processes, and so forth. Let me give you a simple example to illustrate what I mean.

During one session Bob recounted a day he had spent taking his mother, who had chronic arthritis, to the doctor and sitting with her while she complained bitterly to the doctor about her pains and also about how her son, Bob, had repeatedly and consistently neglected her throughout all the years of her illness. Although Bob knew that her account of him was not true, and he tried to correct her, his mother never even acknowledged him and he found himself becoming quite upset and even beginning to doubt his own clear memory of the facts. Later, at the end of the day, his mother had turned to him with a winning smile and told him what a lovely day it had been, how much she had enjoyed spending this pleasant time with him, and how much she loved him.

I asked him how he had felt inside, and he told me he had been confused, distrustful, angry, and upset, not really knowing what was happening or what to believe—his mother's loving words or the terrible turmoil in his gut. Eventually we established that similar events had been going on throughout his childhood, that at times his mother would praise him to the skies and at other times denigrate or abuse him, and that he could never really understand why she did the one rather than the other and could not really believe the praise any more than he could understand the abuse.

Here we have a simple example of discordant reality in which Bob's gut perceptions of his mother's anger and bitterness are totally at odds with the loving words he hears coming from his mother's mouth, words that at other times have evoked warm and positive emotions. He feels confused because he cannot understand why his mother had been so abusive to him in the presence of the doctor and yet so loving at the end of the day? Should he believe what she was saying now or what she said then? On top of this confusion about the workings of his mother's mind, he feels confused about his own perceptions, thoughts, and feelings, for he cannot reconcile the loving feelings he sometimes felt when she spoke those words with the violent loathing he now feels as she talks to him. Much later we were to learn that he was having unconscious fantasies about being physically violated by her and about mutilating her in return. And consciously he now becomes uncertain about the actual facts of their relationship, how many times he has visited her in the past month, and whether, indeed, he had ever done anything to help her or ever really loved her.

Even in that simple example we can see the complexity of the processes involved and can grasp more clearly the existential insecurity and confusion of the many patients who have grown up with such parents. These patients quite literally do not feel sure they are real or that they have minds and bodies of their own, or that their minds and bodies are functioning properly and can be relied on. Such patients are often unable to trust their relationships or the analytic situation because, in order to trust, we must first have some abiding faith in the coherence, constancy, and continuity of our own minds and bodies and the world in which we exist.

If, for example, we were meteorologists and our weather predictions were frequently incorrect, we might doubt either our instruments or our theory, but we would probably still retain our faith in the predictability of the weather. The patients I am describing are convinced from experience that their instruments are faulty; some also feel that their theory is defective, and the most unfortunate have given up the hope altogether that the world is predictable at all.

A young woman who had the misfortune to grow up with a psychotic mother but who, after enormous effort, had begun to create a rich and enjoyable life for herself, came in and told me the following story with great excitement. On entering my office the day before, she had noticed a bag in the closet that belonged to the previous patient, who was still in session, and she had the passing thought that the patient would forget her bag when she left. And sure enough! When she left after her own session, the other patient's bag was still in the closet—the other patient had forgotten it, just as predicted! For clarity's sake, I will omit all the other meanings that this little enactment entailed and focus simply on her disproportionate enjoyment at finding that her prediction, or ESP, as she jokingly called it, was correct. In the course of trying to understand the meaning of this, she described to me a game that she used to play as a child:

P: Our windows were on the second floor, and I would pull the shade halfway down so I could only see people's feet and lower body. And I would watch them walk along and I would imagine some image of the whole person and then when they got close I would pull up the shade and check to see if I was right. That was my favorite game!

I asked her what that was all about.

P: Well, I was desperate to know. I just didn't think I understood all of the multiplicity of things I observed, and it was like an exercise in teaching myself to see if I could learn. . . . I would make this image of the person and then check to see if I was close to it . . . like a training . . . I wanted always to know, to understand, to make sense of . . . I don't understand that feature in myself.
T: Maybe you were trying to make sense out of the disconnected parts of your mother, trying to see if you could get them to match each other or to match your image of reality?
P: Well, I certainly couldn't make any sense of my mother's irrational rages or her unpredictability. It was continually upsetting to me . . . and I think that there's something about knowing or understanding things that I find very soothing or consoling.

Indeed, this young woman, who had been raised in such an unpredictable and largely psychotic environment, was absolutely thrilled when she could find or create something logical, organized, and coherent around her and, in fact, she later went on to become a professor of philosophy. But it turned out that her playful attempts to put together the chaotic and fragmented parts of her mother and of her perception of reality were only part of the story.

It seemed that the mother had been engaged in a lifelong effort to destroy her daughter's reality by attacking all the links that could make her life meaningful. She harassed her daughter in all areas of her life: her attempts to study, to work, and to make other relationships were ridiculed and actively interfered with. But the patient herself, until the analysis, had just as actively denied her mother's psychosis and maintained the illusion that she could still, even now, win her mother's love if only she could find the proper way to do so. Hence the patient, by her denial, was also attacking the links in her own thinking that would otherwise have led to the inevitable but frightening conclusion that her mother was crazy. These attacks on linking had resulted in a generalized feeling that she did not understand people and could not figure out what made them tick.

The game she had loved as a child turned out to be not only an attempt to put together the fragmented reality that her mother had left her with, but also a restitutive attempt to bind together those parts of her own thoughts and objects that she had defensively split apart. Here we may note again the unconscious attempts of the body–mind to heal itself; for just as Bob practiced yoga in order to counteract the restrictive conditions imposed on him by his father, so this little girl played a game trying to rejoin the meaningful links that her mother had torn apart, a process in which she had defensively colluded.

Although I have spent many years working with patients whose parents were thought disordered and relationally disordered, I have found it uncommon for a patient to broach this topic or even to be consciously aware of it. More often, it is only in the course of relating some familiar incident that the patient may suddenly realize that what was accepted as ordinary in his family was really quite strange indeed. In this respect the situation reminds me of those puzzle pages one finds in children's magazines that show a large illustration with the question: *What's wrong with this picture?* Often the analyst's intervention can be confined to a simple question, "You mean the silverware wasn't organized in some way?"

Out of such little cracks in the cosmic egg may then emerge a familial worldview or state of consciousness that may have had a totally shattering impact on the child. I recall in this connection a patient who even as a young child was accustomed to waking, dressing, and feeding herself and then trying to wake up her drunken mother before going to school. It came as a great surprise for her to learn, many years later, that other children did not have to shake their mothers awake but were instead awakened and cared for *by* their mothers. Similarly, another patient, when asked how he had gotten to sleep as a child, insisted that it was just like everyone else. Whenever he happened to feel tired, he went up to his room, turned on the TV, and watched until he fell asleep. When he awoke in the morning, the TV would still be blaring. He was surprised to learn that most small children of his background were put to bed by their parents at a regular time, often with a book or a song.

These disturbances of regulation in the family system often go unrecognized by the child—because the child is so enmeshed in the family pathology—and are usually accompanied by disturbances of thinking and of implicit relational knowing, as well as disturbances of reality testing. So it may take a very long time before a clear and useful representation of the patient's early years can be established, because he needs to have emerged from the pathological familial state of consciousness in which he is embedded before he can fully understand what was wrong with the first picture of his childhood.

Let me pause here to explain what I mean. Just as people have a "normal" state of consciousness and altered states, such as intoxication, and just as these states develop in complexity over time, so participation in certain groups can engender mutually shared states of consciousness. The examples that immediately come to mind are mother–infant dyads, couples in love, and jazz combos, but larger groups can also share states of consciousness; for example, symphony orchestras, families, and lynch mobs. Observing the clinical phenomenon of a patient who regresses dramatically when he returns to his family over the holidays, we are witnessing a regressive shift in a state of consciousness; that is, the patient feels pulled back toward the shared state and the old parameters that were the norms in his family. This is especially true if the parents have separation issues and are, like Bob's parents, unable to accept differences. Then the family's way of being becomes the only possible way of being, and the child is faced with threats of abandonment should he try to be different or grow up and find his own way.

In such cases, although the child cannot *make sense* out of his parents' mental functioning, he learns that any questioning of their attitudes is forbidden and that there is indeed a prohibition on thinking about thinking. This constraint makes it doubly difficult for the child to feel at ease with his own thinking or to achieve reflective self-awareness, unless he is lucky enough to find a book, a friend, or a teacher outside the family who, in one way or another, may raise questions about the premises of the family system. Although this fortuitous happening may sometimes occur explicitly, often enough it occurs implicitly as it slowly dawns on the child that he feels very different being with this neighbor or with that friend's parents than he does when he is with his own family. As if a miracle has taken place, then a brave new world suddenly comes into view.

But in life as in therapy, I have found that the child or patient must first be able to recognize what happened and to understand what interfered with his ability to think before he can fully resume the interrupted developmental path and start to resolve the conflicts that this detour helped him to avoid. Simply to substitute a more benign therapeutic environment for the pathological family environment is a very big step indeed, but without also being able to question even the more benign therapeutic system, the patient will never be able to achieve the evolved self-awareness that will be the basis for true independence.

That is why, in matters of technique, I find it especially important with these patients not to conceal my thinking processes from them, but, rather, to engage in an effort for us both to think together about each other's thinking. I try, whenever possible, to explain the reasoning behind my comments and interpretations, and, better yet, I allow the patient to witness my mind at work in the process of free-associating or making formulations, so that the interpretation becomes a mutual endeavor and is thereby much improved. It is especially useful for such patients to experience the analyst as he tries to deal with doubt and ambiguity, or as he tries to hold two ideas or two roles in mind at the same time, for it opens up the possibility of the patients doing the same. Most important, since I am implicitly asking my patients to trust me with their minds, I struggle to attain a position where I can trust them with my own mind and feel that I have nothing to hide from them.

For the feeling that one has a mind of one's own is the complex outcome of a long developmental process, some disturbances of which I have tried to touch on. Some of the contradictory elements involved were dramatically underlined for me by a man I once worked with, a professor who, after several years of analysis, revealed his absolute conviction that I used the same paper napkin on the pillow for every patient all day long. We knew that his psychotic mother had collected burnt matches and little pieces of string, but the principal dynamic behind this fantasy was an oceanic state of consciousness that kept him sadomasochistically attached to his mother and to the symbiotic family system. He once told me, "I feel that the world is seamless, that we're all connected by a sticky ocean of glue, and I can't allow any cracks or ruptures or breaks in this medium which holds us all together."

His mother's death had not ruptured this medium nor had his abandonment by his first wife, whom he still continued to support. *Indeed, to help such patients recognize the parental pathology and to help them separate from it is one of the most difficult clinical problems we face.* Interestingly, this seemingly timid professor was, in fact, an intrepid mountain climber who sought, by scaling the highest mountains, to place himself in a position where he could identify all the peaks, passes, and mountain chains and orient himself in relation to them. At this supreme moment he would experience a feeling of well-being and sexual satisfaction and, indeed, when this feeling first occurred at age 11 he had been surprised by a spontaneous sexual orgasm. As it became clearer and clearer that his entire personal and professional life had been one enormous attempt to understand his mother's mind and to separate from her without losing his own mind or destroying hers, he said to me one day,

"You remember how I used to complain that I can't make any judgments, that I don't know where I stand, that I'm dumb? That was a lack of overview, a lack of placement relative to other landmarks. When I'm on top of the mountain, I know that *I'm* exactly here and that *that other mountain* is over there. There's a fantastic pleasure in seeing how it all hangs together, in knowing what is what!"

It was fascinating to observe how this very intelligent man, who had difficulties with both explicit and implicit thinking, began to work his way out of the defensive maternal symbiosis, which he compared to an ocean of glue, by climbing alone to the peak of a mountain from which he could observe the lay of the land and simultaneously experience both his oneness with nature and his separateness. And it was in working through his oneness and separateness in the transference, and especially in our coming to understand each other's minds so that it finally dawned on him that I was simply not that kind of person who would use the same napkin for each patient, that he ultimately was able to win his freedom.

Freud, as we know, always maintained that the ego was first and foremost a body ego. And it turns out that thinking, that proudest achievement of our mind, is also coupled to the body so that disorders of thinking are correlated with disorders of the body ego, with disorders of the ego's self-regulation and especially of the ego's boundaries, that is, with the attachment and separation of one body from another. This insight would not have surprised the Professor, who in some sense had spent his life trying to separate his body from the body of his mother without losing the grounding in reality that the body of the mother first represents.

It seems that the philosophers who believe in coconstruction and those who believe in essentialism are, like the rest of us, still trying to deal with the paradox of how it is possible both to be born of someone's flesh and yet to be separate from her, and how it is possible both to live in one's own experience and yet also to observe oneself from the outside. I have tried in this chapter to open up some perspectives on the varieties of disturbed thinking and how we can deal with them both in ourselves and in our patients.

5

ON GETTING FROM
HERE TO THERE

Doublethink means the power of holding two contradictory
beliefs in one's mind simultaneously, and accepting both of
them [as true].
                        —George Orwell, *Nineteen Eighty-Four*

The test of a first-rate intelligence is the ability to hold two
opposed ideas in the mind at the same time, and still retain
the ability to function.
                        —F. Scott Fitzgerald, *The Crack-Up*

For most of us, the process of getting from here to there is something we do not normally think about because it occurs effortlessly
and without conscious attention. But, for some patients, getting
from here to there is neither effortless nor preconscious—they

---

This chapter was written in collaboration with Phyllis Beren, Ph.D.

cannot take it for granted and it frequently involves them in difficulties that can reach nightmarish proportions.

> When Robert's baby daughter first came home from the hospital, he was initially quite fearful that when she cried she would never stop crying, or that when she laughed she would become uncontrollably manic. He dreamed about a series of masks that changed from the tragic to the comic. When Robert thought about the dream of the tragic and comic masks, he related it to his perceptions of his baby's face. He said, "I don't really understand how it is that I get from crying to smiling, so I have very little faith that the baby will be able to do it either."

Masks, of course, are the symbols of transformation. Whether they are part of a rite of passage from adolescence to adulthood, as in certain tribal ceremonials, or mediate a path from sickness to health, as in certain curative ceremonies or exorcisms, they usually have to do with transitions from one state of being to another. The mask allows for an instantaneous rather than a gradual transition; it disrupts our sense of continuity and may therefore elicit uncanny feelings.

But, for Robert and for many other patients, the normal sense of continuity between crying and smiling had already been disrupted or was never fully established. Robert was a very creative young man who frequently found himself in a state of indecision and desperate anxiety over what to do. He always seemed to be frantically obsessing over a choice between two apparently mutually exclusive alternatives: to leave his marriage or not, to leave his therapy or not, to have a baby or not, to do things his wife wanted that made him feel resentful or to do things that he wanted but that made him feel selfish. These continual, frantic obsessions had led one psychiatrist to the conclusion that Robert had an obsessive-compulsive disorder that should be treated with antidepressants. But the medication itself became the subject of obsessions, and it really did not seem to help much.

At one time Robert was planning a trip abroad and was again obsessing over what seemed to him an impossible choice. "If I take my camera along," he said, "then I can photograph the trip, but I won't be experiencing it—but if I don't take my camera, then I can experience the trip, but I won't have any record of it, and after a while I won't even be sure it ever happened."

The camera is our century's exemplary tool for objectifying everything. Robert was obsessing between going on the trip in a state of objective self-awareness in which he could photograph the trip but not experience it; or going on the trip in a state of subjective awareness in which he could experience it but not objectify it. He was obsessing because he knew from experience that he would have great difficulty shifting back and forth between these two states in the course of the trip and would find it impossible to combine the two. Indeed, the obsessive symptomatology itself was a sign of his inability to integrate or arrive at some homeostasis between these two perspectives. Because of his impaired ability to integrate, he felt unable to deal with ambiguity and was forced to dichotomize every situation into an either–or choice that seemed impossible to resolve. One might say that Robert's subjectivity and objectivity did not inform each other or were split off from each other, so that photographing the landscape was not also to have an experience of it, nor was experiencing it also a way to document it by preserving it in memory.

Robert remembered his own mother as rarely being interested in him and always preoccupied with something else. And, in the course of analysis, after Robert and his wife eventually had a baby, my observation of his mother's behavior with her new granddaughter seemed to confirm his assessment. For example, when left to baby-sit her granddaughter, Robert's mother became so involved in a crossword puzzle that she never heard the baby crying, and when Robert came home the infant was in a blue-faced paroxysm. When mutual-gazing with her granddaughter, his mother seemed oblivious to the infant's rhythms and tended either to override them or to abandon the child when she asserted her own desires. These incidents and many others led us to conclude that Robert's mother had real difficulties in switching her attention appropriately from self to other, or in moving appropriately between subjectivity and objectivity. By objectivity, of course, we mean the ability to self-reflect and also take the other into account.

It became viscerally clear to Robert that his frantic oscillations between subjectivity and objectivity and between either–or dichotomies were related to his mother's difficulties helping him create and sustain a transitional area so that there could be a middle containing these extremes rather than a frightening black hole into which he might fall. Because his caregivers had been either unresponsive or inappropriately responsive, Robert had never learned that he could have an effect on his world, or that he could include himself and the other in a larger experience, or make the transition between himself and the other without losing either his objects or his own self-feelings.

What I am describing is a certain type of splitting: how it occurs developmentally and how one observes it operating in an adult patient. I believe that this splitting occurs in earliest development when, for various reasons, a containing transitional space (Winnicott, 1965, 1971) has not been adequately established. A usable transitional space begins to form as the environmental mother becomes tolerably assimilated to the mother as an object. This space can be disrupted by trauma; in fact, one of the more clinically useful definitions of trauma is the sudden, almost irrevocable shattering of transitional space.

I feel that the creation or recreation of an adequate transitional space is essential to the treatment of adults who were traumatized as children (Winnicott, 1967; Ogden, 1985). As I see it, this transitional space evolves largely through the interpenetration of affects and states of consciousness that leads the patient to experience himself as existing in the mind of another and a benevolent other as existing in his mind. Gradually, by virtue of the patient's ability to tolerate a separate perspective and enjoy playing with it, a usable space evolves in which the interchange of affects and ideas becomes possible and an integration and synthesis begins to occur. This, briefly, is the process I am trying to explicate in the patients I discuss.

Many years later I saw another patient, Patricia, whose chief complaints were about her difficulties with relationships, but whose problems seemed in striking ways to resemble Robert's. Patricia was a very intelligent young woman, gifted both musically and scientifically. Although she chose a scientific career in which she was very successful, she had continued her musical studies and was a sought-after amateur oboist. One day, recounting the history of her musical development, she mentioned that before taking up the oboe—at which she immediately excelled— she had studied the piano for several years but had been only a mediocre pianist.

It soon became clear that her problems with the piano stemmed from her virtual inability to deal with two independent voices played at the same time, an order of functioning that was simply not required for the oboe. Slowly, we began to realize that her difficulty dealing simultaneously with two independent voices applied not only to musical instruments but also to ideas, to affects, and also to self and other, which had been her chief complaint.

To take one example among many: practically every weekend Patricia would become conflicted and emotionally distraught trying to decide whether to spend her time doing her own work or to spend it with her boyfriend. Somehow it did not seem possible to divide the time in some comfortable manner or to make a decision that was not immediately subjected to self-criticism either for being selfish or for abandoning her own interests. Ultimately, over the years, it began to seem that whether the problem presented itself as a difficulty dealing with two independent musical voices or with two contradictory feelings or ideas or with a choice between two situations or between two people, there was some basic quandary about managing these apparent dichotomies.

Patricia's mother appeared to be a borderline woman who had a will of iron and an unshakeable belief in her own infallibility. She could love Patricia only as long as Patricia agreed with her, but any attempt on Patricia's part to offer her own thinking or judgment was met with utter derogation, contempt, and the insistence that the mother's position alone represented the whole truth. While the father seemed to have a somewhat less arbitrary view, he was weak and uninvolved and so did not provide a refuge that might have allowed Patricia to disengage from her mother.

Until she came for therapy Patricia had been in the habit of speaking with her mother several times a day; she had managed to maintain this close and uninterrupted connection by never really disagreeing with her about anything significant. Consciously, she was her mother's admirer, acolyte, and follower. In another, split-off part of herself that took a long time to reach, she feared and hated her mother but felt utterly bereft and disoriented without her. Although she experienced herself as incompetent without her mother, she had in reality received honors in math and science at a university where women were not easily recognized.

It appeared that just as Patricia functioned for her mother as the mother's selfobject, so the mother functioned for Patricia as an idealized object whose loss could precipitate disorientation, despair, and psychic collapse. The measure of the part her mother played in Patricia's overall sense of integrity may be suggested by just two incidents. On a day when her mother refused to answer her phone calls after they had had a slight disagreement, Patricia lost her way while driving, became utterly confused and disoriented, and fell into a panic. On another occasion, when unconscious feelings of hostility made her fear for her mother's safety, she felt that life had lost its meaning and she became depressed.

Slowly, as this tangled web was unraveled in the analysis, it turned out that the most important either–or that had governed Patricia's life was at bottom the choice between living her mother's life while experiencing herself as dead, or living her own life and feeling she had killed her mother. To this unfortunate dilemma she had responded for the first 20 years mostly by living her mother's life while feeling dead herself and then, after analysis began, by attempting sporadically to lead her own life and to deal with the extraordinary anxiety, mourning, and occasional exhilaration that this new behavior caused.

Finally, I will tell you about Sam, a four-and-a-half-year-old boy who was brought by his parents with the chief complaint of uncontrollable temper tantrums. When, for example, they tried to take him outside, he would seem to get "stuck" somewhere in the process. He would become upset and insist on redoing everything; that is, just after getting out the door, he would insist on going back, taking off his coat and hat, putting them on again, and then walking out the door again, and he would insist on repeating the whole procedure, step by step, over and over again. When getting out of a car, he would go through a similar performance of wanting to repeat, many times over, all the steps involved in getting out of the car, and nothing else would satisfy him. The parents were desperate about these compulsions and about the temper tantrums that followed if they did not go along with them.

When Sam first came for therapy, he seemed confused, calling a "he" a "she" and commenting that everything seemed the same, that the dolls were dressed alike, that they all looked the same, and the like. The mother herself seemed overly concerned about showing up on time and managing things in a practical way; she was especially anxious about being extremely fair both to Sam and to his older brother and was preoccupied with not hurting anyone's feelings.

When the mother brought Sam for his second interview, she brought along his older brother and remained with him in the waiting room. Sam seemed more animated, but then he wanted his mother and brother to come in and then wanted his brother to leave. Finally, he wanted his mother to leave, but, then, when it was time to end the session, he asked for a piece of tissue to play with at home. Then he wanted another tissue, and, when his mother said no, he began to plead, "Just one more—I have to have another piece." He refused to leave the office and continued to beg for another tissue. The therapist gave him many tissues, but Sam still wanted more, would not leave the office, and finally became overwhelmed. He was stuck in this awful drama. With tears in his eyes, he pleaded like a little lawyer and was totally confused and disoriented until the therapist said, "I can't give you more tissue, and, even if I did, it wouldn't help you leave. Something is upsetting you, and we want to understand what's happening when you have to go from one place to another. Maybe we can talk about it and understand it." "No!" said Sam, "I need another piece of tissue." After giving him one more tissue, she was finally able gently to help him to leave.

Currently, the mother's father is dying. She feels responsible for his caretaking and is having a hard time managing things. She cannot seem to figure out how to be there for her father while also being there for her children. She feels that she has to take care of everything. This fits in with her developmental history. She did not get much individual attention from her own mother, and she developed precociously in her efforts to keep up with her older siblings. She was left to figure things out for herself, and she has unwittingly repeated this pattern with her own children.

The therapist pointed out to the mother that she seemed to attend to everyone else's needs but not her own. The mother began to think about taking the weekend off and going to visit her father, which she ended up doing. Sam began to calm down. He had in part been acting out his mother's confusion about what to do. The mother could not find a way to manage her own conflicted feelings about being with her dying father or being with her children; they appeared to her as unresolvable dichotomies that she could not handle. Sam was in a similar conflict because, if he ended up "there," then he could not be "here," and, if he stayed "here," then he could not be "there"—the other side always seems to get lost. This loss of the other side of the dichotomy is, of course, connected to the impending loss of the grandfather and to his mother's reactions to loss, but, especially, to Sam's reaction to the loss of his space in his mother's mind.

I have described several patients who seem to have conspicuous trouble of one sort or another in getting from here to there. I was struck by the similarities in these cases and in others I have seen, for example, the patient in chapter 2 who could either give herself sexual pleasure or give her lover sexual pleasure, but not both at the same time. I noticed that each of these patients was struggling with some dichotomy or split and oscillating, sometimes frantically, between each side of the dichotomy. In little Sam's case, the dichotomy was between staying home and going outside, apparently a separation issue; in Patricia's case, it was between living her mother's life or living her own life, apparently a self–other issue; in Robert's case, it was between smiling and crying, apparently a pleasure–pain issue. For most of these patients there were multiple issues at stake, but no matter what the particular issue was, the patients always experienced themselves as being flung back and forth between extremes or within dichotomies, unable to find some higher level of integration that might allow a smooth transition between them. Many of these patients also had difficulties multitasking and complained about not being able to do more than one thing at a time.

Phenomenologically, they all seemed to feel like a traumatized deer caught in the headlights, unable to decide what to do and prone to making rapid and self-destructive movements. They all seemed unable to think their way out of whatever dichotomies or opposing pulls they were experiencing, and they were attempting to fill the breach by relying on some external help, a person, a thing, or a ritual to help as a transitional object, just as little Sam kept asking pathetically for more and more tissue as a kind of concrete connection to enable him to span the gap or to get from here to there.

Their experience, in its most extreme form, was like jumping across a deep chasm while not being able to see the other side nor even to be sure that it was there at all—people were urging them to jump, but they felt as if they would be jumping into the void. Once on the other side, it would be equally frightening to jump back because, in their experience, the other side was all but unreachable or else it had entirely disappeared. Little Sam felt this way about going outside or coming back in again; Patricia felt that way about playing two independent voices simultaneously on the piano and about spending time with her mother or spending time by herself; Robert felt that way about objectifying his trip with photographs while not experiencing it, or experiencing it without having a record to enable him to know that he had taken the trip. He also suffered this way over how he and his daughter could get from smiling to crying; there was either one emotion or its polar opposite, and when he was immersed in one there was no way of getting to the other or even of remembering it in a practically useful way. How to find the other side? And how to find the way from one to the other or the ground that joins them?

Although these problems seem related to Kris's (1985) divergent conflicts or conflicts of ambivalence, I felt that what I was seeing was more akin to trauma or the aftereffects of cumulative traumas. In the patients I observed, the ego seemed to be momentarily overwhelmed by anxiety and to have never fully developed or to have lost its mediating capacity. The result was a kind of helplessness verging on panic. Some patients felt themselves to be in an altered state; some experienced a loss of self or a loss of agency; and all looked for a specific kind of help—they needed to be held or soothed or actually told what to do in order to get "unstuck" and move from here to there.

Interestingly, in the child material of which Sam was but one example, when the child turned to the mother for help, it seemed that most of the time the mother also did not know what to do, as well-meaning or attentive as she might be. In guidance sessions, the mother was often eager to learn what to do, and it usually turned out that she herself had suffered as a child from a similar lack of knowledgeable parenting. These mothers were not mindful of what had happened to them in their own childhood (Coates, 1998), nor were they reflectively aware of what they were doing with their children (Fonagy et al., 1991; Main and Hesse, 1992).

In attempting to clarify my thinking about this, I noted some similarities observed in all these child and adult patients:

1. They all had an exceptional degree of difficulty with self-constancy and object constancy in one way or another.

2. They all had some evident degree of difficulty with states of subjective awareness (feeling vital and alive), with states of objective or reflective self-awareness (being able to reflect on oneself while taking the other into account), or both, as well as particular difficulty with the transitions between these two states and their integration.

3. They all were subject to states of high anxiety and, when in such states, they tended to experience their world in extremes or as either–or dichotomies. This experience terrified them because there seemed to be no way of integrating these dichotomies or splits and no intermediate ground to join or connect them.

I observed that all these patients, in certain states of consciousness, were unable usefully to visualize, to remember, or to hold and contain in a larger context the other side of the polarized state, whether the dichotomy was self–other, attachment–separation, pleasure–pain, or even being alive or dead. It was as if they could deal only with one side at a time, just as Patricia was unable to deal with two independent voices simultaneously on the piano. In some way or to some varying degree the other side or voice is either dimly perceived but cannot be dealt with or, sometimes, it seems to be intermittently forgotten or even obliterated. They could not master the "paradox of simultaneity" (Benjamin, 1988).

I understand this narrowing of perspective to be related to the absence or deficiency of a usable transitional area in which dichotomy, ambiguity, and paradox can be acknowledged and contained (Winnicott, 1968). Fundamentally, something seemed to have gone wrong with the dialectics of the self, with the relations of the self to other selves, with the mutual sharing of states of consciousness, and with the interpenetration of affects. Normally, the mother recognizes her child's state of being by means of her emotional resonance with the child, her passionate observation, and empathy. She imagines and recognizes her child's *true self,* which "is in part fashioned by the quantitative and gradually qualitative aspects of endogenous states (stimulation level, sensitivities, inhibitory tendencies, activity levels, etc.)" (Ellman, in press). The mother recognizes and responds to the infant's physical and emotional states, and she and the child metabolize each other's affects and perceptions through a process of *interpenetration* (e.g., Balint, 1960; Loewald, 1980; Grunes, 1984, 1998; Ellman, in press). The mother's recognition, containment, management, and verbalization of her baby's states, and the baby's complementary responses to the mother, form the mechanism by which development normally proceeds. In the cases that I have been discussing, this mechanism was tragically compromised, because of the mother's difficulties recognizing and responding appropriately to her child, because the child was so extremely high- or low-drive that few mothers could have responded adequately, or because in some other way child and mother are essentially mismatched.

Certain infants with exceptionally high or low levels of endogenous stimulation or extraordinary sensitivities may be very difficult for the mother to understand and to contain. High-endogenous-state infants may experience even mild additional stimulation as aversive, whereas low-state infants may need more stimulation than is readily available in order for them to feel alive. I recall a high-drive patient who was notoriously difficult to soothe as an infant and was experienced as a constant torment by his mother. As an adult he felt an almost continual need for soothing through indiscriminate sex, in which he indulged almost daily. This type of state mismatch between child and caregiver is a fertile breeding ground for the kind of sadomasochistic pathology described in chapter 7.

It seems that the dichotomies and splits my patients were struggling with often arose as a response to some faulty recognition or containment, such as the many varieties of flawed responses I have enumerated. It occurred to me that, although we tend to think of many of the polarities of life—self–other, attachment–separation, activity–passivity, pleasure–pain, and so forth—as objectively dichotomous, they need not necessarily be *experienced* as such in normal development and sometimes may not be, provided that the developmental stage is being appropriately managed and contained (Aron, 2001). Certain theorists (e.g., Kohut, 1977) believe that seeing the oedipal as being an extremely anxious, violent, and narcissistically wounding phase may be a view of its pathological development as a result of inappropriate environmental responses, and that normal development may, in fact, proceed considerably more smoothly.

While observing these patients' frantic oscillations between dichotomies, I became convinced that not only the oscillations but also the experience of the dichotomy itself might be the result of a pathological process. I suspect that an experience of irresolvable dichotomy or splitting is generated when a child confronts a new emotional experience, arising internally or externally, that is not being adequately recognized, contained, or managed by the environmental mother. If inadequately managed experiences occur frequently, and if the mismanagement is severe enough, they result in a cumulative trauma rather than an integrated learning experience and will lead to dichotomization and splitting. One might say that adequately managed occurrences lead to continuous, or analog, experiences, whereas inadequately managed occurrences lead to discontinuous, or digital, experiences.

When the mother is able to help the child manage, contain, and eventually verbalize new experience, whether internal or external, then the child has a relatively seamless experience that can be continuously symbolized, lays the groundwork for a transitional area, and encourages a sense of agency. When the mother is unable to help the child adequately contain new experience, then a traumatic situation arises that may lead to splitting and dichotomization, and one might view the ensuing oscillations between extremes as the child's desperate attempts to gain equilibrium or to regain a pretraumatic homeostasis.

It seems to me that in normal development the mother helps the baby feel that he is alive in her mind through her recognition, containment, and management of her baby's states through the interpenetration of their affects and their growing reflective self-awareness (Bach, 1985, 1994), mentalization (Fonagy et al., 1991, 2002), and mindfulness of each other. I believe that transitional space cannot develop in the baby's mind unless he feels that he lives in the mind of his mother or his primary caregiver. I also feel that it can be severely traumatic for the child to experience himself as not being held or not being alive in his mother's mind. This feels to him as if he were unseen, unheard, unrecognized, unacknowledged, and totally abandoned—as if he were dying or dead. Children who suddenly no longer feel alive in their mother's mind may experience this loss quite literally as being dropped, falling endlessly, being split into a million parts or atomized, or disappearing entirely.

Some adult patients may occasionally remember such experiences from their childhood, and many adult patients in a regressive transference report similar traumatic experiences when they feel, for whatever reason, that they have dropped out of their analyst's mind. In certain cases this may give rise to retaliatory rage and attacks on linking, whereas in other cases one finds hopelessness, loss of vitality, and despair at ever being able to repair the rift or regain some place in another's mind. Under such circumstances, dichotomies and splits of whatever kind seem insurmountable and therefore terrifying and sometimes persecutory. Thus the condition that makes dichotomization and splitting a relatively permanent process is one in which the child does not feel reliably present in another's mind and when he cannot trust that his affects will be accepted without retaliation and returned in a suitably metabolized form.

By contrast, when a child feels held by his mother and alive in her mind, then dichotomies and even prior splits feel less terrifying and more easily manageable. One might say that the child identifies with and learns from his mother's ability to contain and synthesize or metabolize disparate elements. When the child knows that he exists in his mother's mind, then he feels that self and other have touched each other and interpenetrated and that each can survive. In the transitional space that develops in the child's mind, opposites can touch one another and they can playfully coexist in each other's presence.

In the widest view, splitting appears to develop through some extreme disjunction between the needs of the child and the needs of the caregiver, a disjunction that the child experiences as a state of traumatic detachment from his caregiver. I should, of course, re-emphasize that I am seeing all this from the child's vantage point; some parents who would be objectively good enough for most children may be experienced as traumatically insufficient by certain children with very special needs.

Since from another point of view problems of polarization and splitting can be seen as related to attentional difficulties, I wondered if they might be connected to issues of multitasking. Interestingly, although both Robert and Patricia had presented with conflicts about being involved with more than one thing at a time, as I examined Patricia's current interactions with her mother I noticed that the mother herself seemed to have difficulty with holding more than one person in mind at the same time.

Bruner (1968) has studied the ability of infants to accept more than one item being handed to them. This ability increases with age as children, with both hands full, find nooks and crannies in and around their bodies to store additional items. Bruner has seen this as the ability to have a psychic reserve or store items mentally and connected it to the ability to pay attention to one thing while keeping something or someone else in the back of one's mind. It seems that this ability is crucial for parents to possess and for children to learn, for even an ideal mother cannot possibly keep one child at the center of her attention all the time.

I have found, though, that there are extraordinary differences between parents in this regard, differences to which children are acutely sensitive. In my experience, a child immediately *knows* the difference between a mother whose attention is elsewhere but who keeps him in the back of her mind and a mother who has let the child drop out of her mind completely. When a child senses that he has been emotionally forgotten or dropped out of his mother's mind he feels annihilated (see chapter 1). In the best of cases, he is distraught but keeps trying to get back in; in the worst of cases, he feels doomed, as if he has been dropped and is falling endlessly into a bottomless black hole.

We can imagine an interpenetrative process where a mother holds her child in mind while attending to something else, contrasted with a splitting process where the mother completely drops or affectively abandons the child. This contrast may seem analogous to an experience sometimes encountered by therapists, when an adult narcissistic patient, whom you have been seeing for some time and to whom you have become attached, walks into your office and announces without warning that this will be his last session. The shock that you feel on hearing this news is an extremely pale version of the trauma the child must experience when confronted with a parent who has split him off from her psychic reality.

Little Sam was not so much feeling utterly cut off from his mother, who was basically a caring and attentive person, as he was reacting to a situational stressor that had diverted the mother's attention to her dying father. You will recall, however, that the mother herself had difficulty dealing with dichotomies or ambivalence and that she herself had not experienced an adequate dependent phase but had grown up as a precocious child who was obliged to figure too much out for herself. Typically, she had not developed the mindfulness or self-awareness about her own experience that might have enabled her to assimilate it better, and when she brought up her own children she expected them to learn mostly on their own, as she had. Sam, who was not fully toilet trained, needed more help from her but she was loathe to give it, partly out of fear of being intrusive. I also understood her exaggerated emphasis on being fair to both siblings as an overcompensation for her endopsychically perceived difficulty in holding one child in mind while attending to the other. She seemed to be unconsciously afraid that if she attended to one sibling she might drop the other, just as she consciously feared that if she attended to her dying father she might ignore her children. Certain hints in the interviews led me to assume that this had been her own experience in childhood.

It seems that we are all continually engaged in the project of integrating body and mind, subject and object, and process and content; that we are always occupied, on a variety of levels, with pulling things together and making sense out of the disparate elements in our lives. The outlines of this project become clearly visible only when they are least successful—when, for example, someone has chronic trouble getting from here to there.

Because a person's sense of self is a unifying vision, to do less than see the polarities and paradoxes of life in terms of this vision is somehow to distort essential elements of the human situation. Perhaps it is possible that in earlier times or in other cultures a unifying vision of the world that included our place within it was easier to achieve. But many of the patients we see today have severe or chronic difficulties maintaining their sense of self while functioning within multiple frameworks, or while shifting between levels of meaning, symbolism, and reality.

As analysts we find ourselves engaged with certain patients in an ongoing effort to provide the recognition and containment that was missing in their development; to provide a space in which confusion and ambiguity can be tolerated and explored and in which raw, polarized emotions can be metabolized and eventually integrated. And as analysts we find meaning in devoting our lives to being useful to our patients and in helping our patients find meaning in their own lives by being useful to us, to someone close to them, and especially to themselves.

6

CONFUSION IN THE
ANALYTIC HOUR

Categories and conceptual systems are necessary both to define our world and to give it stability, but at the same time they imprison us and make it difficult for us even to imagine perspectives that go beyond the schemas of our experience. I think it was Alfred North Whitehead who once remarked that if you want to understand a culture deeply, you should try to grasp what nobody in that culture talks about, that is, what everybody takes for granted. And Marx, of course, maintained that ideology is a viewpoint determined by the economic powers of the time, but a viewpoint that strikes its adherents as self-evident, the unquestioned nature of things, and as the one and only way that reality can be perceived. When the conceptual system or the ideology is collapsing, or when the adherent of a cult is being deprogrammed, then the true believer finds himself in a state of profound confusion, caught between conflicting worldviews and often unable to know whether what he is thinking are his own thoughts or thoughts that have been put into him.

Dysfunctional family systems are like cults, and the patients who come out of them, often emerge with similar questions about the nature of the world and the reality of their own thoughts. They have lost confidence and trust not only in other people, but also in the reliability of their own judgment and the validity of their way of thinking.

Some years ago I (Bach, 1984) wrote about a patient, Peter, whose confidence in the validity of his own thinking was so fragile that, as the transference grew more and more intense, he could no longer allow me to speak a single word because he felt that my words would overwhelm his own precarious thoughts and would violate and destroy his mind. I recounted how my many different attempts to analyze this dynamic resulted only in Peter's responding as if I actually were trying to brainwash or destroy him. Finally, seeing no alternative and with the greatest reluctance and difficulty, I lapsed into a silence that lasted for more than a year. During that time Peter continued to come for each hour, to associate, and to analyze on his own, in my silent presence. Every few days or months I would try to say something to test the waters, but my least utterance seemed so terrifying to him, had such severe and prolonged negative effects, and caused such rage and confusion that eventually I returned to complete silence. I have elaborated elsewhere (1985) on the hatred, sadism, and love buried in this transference and countertransference and will not go into it here. One day, long after I had largely given up hope that this treatment could ever work out, Peter mentioned a dream, which he had done many times before, but this time he asked me what I thought about it, and we went on to talk almost as if nothing unusual had ever happened and it had not been over a year since our last two-way conversation. Retrospectively, we were able to analyze some of what all this meant, but I now wonder whether that hour of the dream was the "good" hour, or whether all the silent hours were the "good" hours, or whether there is something wrong with thinking about it in this way.

In any event, I became interested in the gaps among a patient's reality, the reality in his dysfunctional family, and the various levels of reality in the therapeutic situation. Typically, these gaps are characterized by states of confusion, and as confusion in the transference is often accompanied by confusion in the countertransference, at its height the situation may resemble Tolstoy's (1869) descriptions in *War and Peace*, where, in the heat of battle, the soldiers have no clear idea of what is going on and even the generals cannot really be sure of what is happening. Eventually, the fog lifts and the situation clarifies. If we are lucky, we have managed to survive to fight another day.

Of course, I am portraying the extremes of the work with the most challenging patients, but even with more moderate cases moments of confusion may occur when, for example, the patient insists that we have said or done something that we ourselves might not be absolutely certain about and it slowly dawns on us that we have touched the limits of our systems of mutual confidence and certainty and are now on the very outer edges, where trust has become a vital factor.

My patient Peter had never known his father; his mother was psychotic; and his sister, who was 15 years older than him, had been a kind of surrogate mother until her sudden death when Peter was in his 20s. Two previous treatments had failed, but because I came highly recommended Peter had started his third treatment with a very idealized belief in my abilities and had begun by welcoming my interventions and interpretations until an increasing regression into a negative maternal transference had led to the impasse I described. After we began talking again, we were able to reflect on what had occurred, which gave both of us some confidence that at least we had not betrayed our assigned functions and that we had neither murdered nor abandoned one another. I would not say that we fully trusted each other, for complete trust goes beyond what we had, which was more like a confidence that each of us would try to fulfill his role in our relationship to the best of his abilities. But this in itself, as you have seen, was difficult enough to achieve.

But even after we began talking again, confusion was still rampant in the analytic setting. Peter began to be confused about the time of his sessions and the location of my office, facts that had never perplexed him before. Although he mostly managed to show up, it was with an air of disbelief that I would really be there or really be expecting him. Ultimately, it became clear that this confusion and disbelief in the transference led back to a confusion about his mother's mental functioning—questions about how to understand her or read her mind and whether or not he could trust it. If he could not trust his mother's mind, then he certainly could not trust his own mind or mine. Part of his confusion about time and location was a function and display of how utterly disoriented he felt when he stood, as he did now, with one foot in his mother's world and one foot in the transference world with me. And, although I usually seemed to know the location of my own office and the hours we were supposed to meet, we eventually managed to confuse the situation to such an extent that at times I too became unsure about when our appointments were scheduled.

Adding to this muddle, Peter had moved out of the family home during the time of the Great Silence, and he now seemed on the verge of having a girlfriend. I am reporting here a very ordinary hour in which nothing dramatic seemed to occur and in which, as it happened, I said scarcely a word but nevertheless felt very present, related to, and emotionally touched, in contrast to the silent hours of the previous year, which I had experienced as sadistically controlling and unrelated to me as a person.

One day he came to a session and began by saying,

I'm not sure what I'm going to talk about[1] . . . there are a lot of different topics . . . as if I'm going to ask you what you think I should do . . . but how would you know? Last night I was talking with Joe about all the stuff going on . . . I realized I keep arguing this one point because the other consultant said something . . . but this may be the wrong topic altogether. . . . There was this thing happened Friday . . . I was avoiding this, but was thinking about it coming over . . . thinking to ask you, but you wouldn't . . . I think you couldn't know . . .

We had a party for Jocelyn before she left, and she acted weird—at least I think she did. Last year at the annual party, she acted weird and looked away, and I thought to myself she's just shy, but I don't know. . . . But this time it happened again, and I thought maybe there's something she's angry at, and it didn't seem to make that much sense. . . . I guess I started feeling maybe she didn't like me . . .

And there's this whole thing that happened with Robert, where he pretends one thing and means something else. . . . These are like little signals that are suddenly popping up. . . . Now I'm thinking that at times with Robert I felt like it was a misunderstanding . . . but then I do tend to think of myself and not about other people . . .

---

[1]Ellipses indicate pauses.

I guess maybe it's about this guy at work, and it ended up in a great fight with the boss . . . you could tell when the boss spoke that there had been a lot of trouble . . . I heard one thing . . . there had been a lot of fighting. . . . Then I was always complaining about the kids, and there was lots of fighting. Jocelyn was always listening, but maybe she didn't like it. . . . It doesn't make sense. Why would she for so many years be so available? She didn't have to invite me out for dinner or to meetings. . . . Somehow I started blaming myself . . . like somehow I was the cause of all the trouble . . . but it still doesn't make sense . . . it's like . . . I guess . . . I'm also thinking . . . I skipped something. . . . Maybe she was trying to protect me around issues with the kids, and there was this big fight . . . my behavior embarrassed her and . . . I guess I'm making this all up . . . and that somehow she felt betrayed by me . . . and I'm somehow filling in . . . that somehow all of us were insulted. . . . One person said, "You shouldn't have young people like that doing the job," . . . so I think I took it as if I'm not really qualified . . . and I don't think it's true, but it goes to my self-doubts and inadequacies. . . . Of course, I don't have a degree like some other people, so that gets mixed up or stirred up. . . . My thought is . . . I'm more thorough . . . I spend more time . . . I'm more tuned into the kids, but it's not really true . . .

What I'm saying doesn't fit the rest of my perceptions . . .

Maybe I'm so awkward that she gets awkward 'cause I get very awkward. . . . [Peter is crying now] Everybody was speaking, so, when Morton spoke and said something about missing her at the end, and Jocelyn indicated that she would see him again . . . I'm listening to this feeling jealous and . . . Morton is very good at saying positive things . . . we were at lunch one time, and he mentioned how to handle Elizabeth. . . . I don't know how to do it . . . so I took it for granted that Jocelyn knew how I felt . . . I do that with the kids too . . . I don't tell them that this is very good . . . I'm only critical with them . . . and then Sara spoke and said nice things, and she said she'd been a joy to work with . . . and then I went to her, but she kept turning away. . . . One time I saw her staring at the boss and thought it was a bad time . . . I finally went up to her and tried to say something, but . . .

I don't know . . . I'd already written something that was more direct, but I never finished it 'cause there were people behind me . . . there was a sentence that I left out, and then she responded to it, but it was in the same vein . . . awkward . . . it wasn't as heartfelt as I would have wanted . . . and I remember she had her hand on my shoulder. . . . I don't remember how that happened . . . she must have . . . I don't think I would have started that . . .

And I'm having also a memory of this scene with Esther, 'cause she was crying and talking about being sick, and I did take her hand, and I did a little better with her, but it's the same awkwardness. . . . You can hear it in how she's speaking, but this time I was able to be more direct . . . and I was crying, of course, but that was okay . . . we were in her room alone, and she was crying, and there was a moment where I wanted to say I love you, and it went by, but I had said something before that. . . . She was talking about how she didn't want to leave us [Peter is crying] and how bad she felt, but she was also feeling guilty. . . . She had all these feelings about separation, and I got very upset. . . . I'm trying to remember what I said . . . I think I said that I felt the same way . . . that I didn't want her to leave and that I would miss her . . .

I'm just thinking how with Robert I couldn't say anything, but then it ended up totally different, but then I thought he was coming back, but he's not coming back. . . . I can understand with Robert why he doesn't say good-bye and that he doesn't make phone calls . . .

But for me to say something . . . of course, the other person I think of is my sister lying on the bed in the hospital, and I just couldn't say anything, and obviously she couldn't say anything, and that's where it was. . . . There was this sentence about how disappointed she was . . . everybody was doing well . . . which I then figured out meant that she wished she could have stayed to finish the job . . . she felt it was unfinished, which was true . . . and that we still needed her, and I can see Jocelyn, she's very maternal, and Sara was saying that she was like a kid, and she took care of her, and it's true . . . she doesn't have any children, and she loves animals, and she told me about her niece who has a dog, and she visits all the time . . . and someone said how she was always able to care about the kids and also care about the teachers . . . so she probably felt that way about me . . . you know I just start making things up . . .

But I guess my sister was also like that because, you know, she didn't say anything much, and I was remembering how when I was little I discovered a puppy near the house. . . . It didn't belong to anyone, and I ended up taking care of him . . . I remember how I fed the puppy, and I know I was always very nurturing, which I think came from my sister 'cause my mother's reaction was to be very disgusted, and obviously that's not how my sister felt . . . she encouraged that kind of thing . . . and I guess it's similar in a way to Jocelyn, 'cause she doesn't get disgusted by people. . . . People do things, and you could be very judgmental and disgusted by people, but that's never how she responds. . . . It would be hard to imagine that that's what she's doing with me . . . and I think that's why I'm so involved with Lynne, 'cause she's able to be very articulate about it . . . always supportive and overlooking bad things or understanding where it comes from and not being judgmental . . .

So I don't know if I can do anything, but probably the best approach would be . . . should I ask her why she's mad at me . . . but I don't think she's mad at me . . . I know I'm not very good at this . . . to try to force myself to do something I really can't do is not a good thing . . .

Maybe just to understand the situation better . . . that's what I should do . . . just try to understand it.

Perhaps you found this verbatim record somewhat confusing, with its large cast of characters, fluid associations, and strong nonverbal component, because Peter is crying throughout much of the session. The session is *about* confusion, about not knowing how to understand people's motivations, about not knowing how to act with people, and about not knowing how to express loving feelings. Peter is crying because he has become acutely aware of his deficiencies and their consequence, and he is mourning his incapacities and his lost opportunities. He also keeps struggling with the urge to ask me to explain Jocelyn's behavior or to tell him what to do about it, but he keeps coming back to the understanding that he knows her better than I do and that I do not have any magical solutions. His psychotic mother always had the answer to everything, and it has taken Peter many years to discover how intrusive and out of touch with reality she was, and finally to begin to emerge from his total involvement with the family cult.

His early inclination to idealize my words had been followed by a total resistance to hearing any words that I had to say. After we overcame this impasse, he slowly reached a point where he could usually distinguish what he felt was in his mind from whatever I might be saying, but he was still very afraid of losing this tenuous hold on his own reality. In this hour Peter eventually found the right answer for himself, and the right answer, in this context, was just to try to understand things better. But it has taken years of work for him to be able to arrive at this simple conclusion because, for Peter, coming from a family where psychotic acting out was the order of the day, the option of trying to understand things or engaging in any kind of self-reflection was a strange, unheard of, and therefore unimaginable possibility.

A few months later, Peter mentioned that being able to express his love and appreciation to Jocelyn for being his mentor was really just like being able to express his feelings for me; and he told me quite simply that our work together had restored his ability to think. As he explained about the year of enforced silence,

> At first I had to keep you absolutely quiet because any word you said destroyed all my thoughts, but later I just needed you too much to get angry at you. . . . It was like a lifeline . . . I could get into myself only when I was here, and I needed that in order to connect to myself . . . in order to know what I was feeling, and I don't know what would have happened without that, and I wasn't willing to give that up . . . I wasn't able to . . . you see, to have an argument is really to assume that it's okay to be separate, and I didn't believe that was the case . . . it never was the case with my mother. . . . You know, I keep crying, and yesterday I was talking about needing Jocelyn and losing her, and now I've said the same thing about you basically.

And I must admit that only at this point did I suddenly realize that Peter, whom I had often thought of as a chronic and interminable patient, was going to get better and have a real termination and a real life. In fact, it took another two or three years before this happened, but eventually Peter moved to another place, got married, and started a family. I still hear about how he is doing from an occasional letter. I suppose that, after all, this was a good hour because it made clear that essentially Peter had learned to trust me with the contents of his mind without needing to project things into me or fearing that I would project my things into him in a way that would destroy him.

What did I learn from this experience?

First of all, that just as Peter was imprisoned within his family psychosis where a self-reflective, nonsadistic, and nonparanoid internal world was unthinkable, I also was imprisoned within my own world and my psychoanalytic training so that a treatment in which I was obliged to remain silent, not for an hour or even a week, but possibly for years on end, was equally unthinkable and unacceptable. At different stages I found this enforced silence sadistically controlling, personally humiliating, and almost uncontrollably infuriating. As Peter was on the couch and talking, I would occasionally invent things to do that distracted me from listening, but doing this was seldom gratifying. At times I was convinced that the only ethical thing to do was to stop the treatment immediately; at other times I did not care about ethics but just wanted to get rid of him; and at still other times I sank into a masochistic submission that cloaked very sadistic feelings about how many dollars per minute I was getting paid—but really no amount of dollars could be worth this torture. After a very long time of working these feelings through mostly on my own, because I was too embarrassed to disclose this treatment in its entirety to almost anyone, I reached a state of narcissistic equilibrium in which my feelings of shame, loathing, and rage and my sadomasochism had somehow been sufficiently worked through so that I could begin to listen to what Peter was saying in a more calm and open way, maybe not without any preconceptions but at least with different preconceptions than before.

Meanwhile, Peter seemed to be going through a similar evolution. Feelings of being controlled by me, of having his thoughts erased by me, of his insignificance compared with my greatness, of my contempt for him and my not really caring for him alternated with rage at me for not wanting to listen to him—why couldn't I just shut up when he asks me to? It's easy enough, and he's paying me for it. I can't really understand what he needs, I'm just tolerating him, I must hate him, I'm going to drive him crazy like his mother, or he's going to drive me crazy, and then I'll disappear like his father and sister. And at times he was ashamed to be crying in front of me and humiliated that he hated me and yet needed me at the same time.

In a way we were both struggling with similar problems. And, strangely, the very long time that we spent not being able to talk to each other about these problems did not seem to have impeded the treatment. Sometimes I would feel like Peter, unable to clarify my confused emotions or to know how to talk about them; at other times I seemed to be Peter's mother, filled with an ambivalent hatred and love that bound us together in a sadomasochistic coupling so that it was only by losing my voice completely that Peter would be able to find his. At times I could see this situation clearly, but at other times it was obscured by an array of feelings ranging from boredom to fury. Indeed, the lack of verbal interaction highlighted the importance of countertransference analysis that I feel is such a crucial part of working with disturbed patients. It also highlighted how we were constantly in affective communication—observing, containing, metabolizing, and responding to each other's feelings. Peter would sometimes puzzle or comment about how I seemed to be feeling but would never ask for verification, and it was through this window that I eventually saw how much trouble he must have had from early on reading and understanding his mother's mind.

I now also recall that over the year of this protracted silence we did, in fact, talk to each other a number of times at the beginning or end of some hours. We spoke about appointment changes or vacation arrangements, which we handled in a perfectly rational and mutually agreeable way, but Peter was always off the couch at the time and had somehow made it clear that his insistence on unilateral silence applied only to the analytic condition. Somehow his stance also clarified that we each had a life of our own in other domains and that the madness we were going through together was an analytic creation that was only one of a number of possible realities.

Later on in the treatment, of course, we talked to each other in an ordinary way, and I made some interpretations from time to time, some of which seemed helpful but others seeming to serve more to test the limits of my own understanding or to make sure we were both on the same track. Nevertheless, it seemed of great importance to verbalize certain aspects of our relationship even though we both were aware of them, if only to demonstrate that I was able to speak them and that he was able to hear them—that a symbolic space had been created in which the two of us could usefully live together.

I began this chapter by maintaining that dysfunctional families are like cults. Cult members are imprisoned, as we all are, within the categories and systems of attitudes and points of view that underwrite their reality and ways of thinking, and when a patient emerges from such a family into the world, he often finds himself in a state of confusion not only about his sense of reality but even about whether his thoughts originate in himself or in someone else. Such was the case with Peter, who found it necessary to silence me completely in order to guarantee the integrity of his own thinking. But while this example is certainly extreme, this kind of problem is not atypical with challenging patients.

I am sure that we have all had patients whose views of reality seemed different from ours and perhaps even repugnant to ours: racist, sexist, fascist, sadistic, exploitative, psychopathic, or just far out. Inevitably this problematic of difference enters the transference arena and has the potential to become an ongoing sado-masochistic battle over whose perception of reality is correct. Here we are talking not only about thought processes but also about emotional and regulatory processes: Is the consulting room too warm or too cold, too light or too dark? Is the analyst too rigid or too labile, too early or too late, too verbal or too silent?

Normally we work these issues out collaboratively with the patient by understanding their deeper transferential meanings, but if the patient, like Peter, seems unable to cooperate then we may still try to collaborate with him by going along with his vision of reality even when he rejects ours. As Peter taught me, some patients cannot really experience themselves as completely separate in the transference regression, and so they cannot believe in or coexist with separate psychic realities. The idea that the same reality can be viewed in different ways by different people, and that the patient's *and* the analyst's views can each have truth and legitimacy is often beyond the patient's emotional comprehension and is also sometimes very difficult for us to comprehend as well. A true collaboration between two independent people may be impossible, and we must defer to the patient's vision of reality until he becomes better able to tolerate our presence and our psychic reality in the room with him.

Whether we deal with words, concepts, categories, or regulatory processes, there will usually be areas where some clash or conflict emerges between those concepts and processes that seem completely natural and unquestionable to the patient and those concepts and processes that seem completely natural and unquestionable to the analyst. In the end, we find ourselves involved in creating transitional areas or demilitarized zones between the slowly revealed basic concepts of the patient's cult and the slowly revealed basic concepts of our own cult. These demilitarized zones are important not only because within them we have agreed not to kill each other, but also because they can slowly become transitional areas where we share the sense that it does not really matter who said what or where things might eventually lead. Demilitarized zones change into transitional areas and then into transitional space where trust becomes possible. And once trust is possible, then playing together becomes possible, and at this point we and the patient are well on our way to recognizing the existence of multiple realities for both patient and analyst, multiple realities that can each be recognized and accepted as having its own legitimacy and authenticity.

Thus it may be that in each true analytic process, both analyst and patient come to understand that *the same reality can be viewed in different ways by different people and that the patient's point of view and the analyst's point of view can both have a certain reality and legitimacy.* I reiterate this point because I now believe that even experienced analysts must learn it over and over again. We need to relearn and relearn partly because we all live in different worlds and partly because the multiple realities inherent in the psychoanalytic situation make for great difficulty in shifting between various levels of meaning, symbolism and reality. And it is precisely at these transitions, or shifts between levels, contexts, and frameworks, that most transference disruptions occur. But it is also here that the greatest potential exists for changes in both parties.

So Peter and I eventually found our way to some mutual trust and understanding and were able to look back with a certain equanimity at that time when we were both boiling together in the cauldron of the transference. Not that I believe that psychoanalysis need always be such an intensely scalding process, for sometimes, if both analyst and patient have attained a level of symbolic development where words have mutually accepted meanings and are connected to authentic emotions, even in the transference, then it may work out in a far easier and less disruptive way than it did in this encounter. But entering the inmost world of another human being is always a descent into the Inferno, an adventure for which we can never be entirely prepared and in which anything might happen and our most cherished beliefs be suddenly put to the question. For, as Proust reminds us, those ideas that seem clearest to us are the ones that have the same degree of confusion as our own.

7

SADOMASOCHISM IN CLINICAL PRACTICE AND EVERYDAY LIFE

Franz Kafka is said to have observed that the primary fact of childhood is the slow, constant, and forcible induction of the child into the great lie, by which he meant the hypocrisy of civilization.

Freud (1930), of course, had made a related observation when he suggested that civilization engenders discontent because the civilizing process relies on the repression of instincts or needs that will thereafter always seek expression and satisfaction.

But Freud (1924) suggested an alternative to either totally rejecting the great lie of civilization or sporadically rebelling against it. He felt that the ego could, by deforming *itself*, avoid a direct confrontation between its own needs and the demands of civilization. "In this way," he concluded, "the inconsistencies, eccentricities and follies of men would appear in a similar light to their sexual perversions, through the acceptance of which they spare themselves repressions" (pp. 152–153).

The socialization of the child begins from the day of its birth, and each phase of development builds on previous phases in a transformative way. In our own culture one of the key periods of forcible socialization of the child is the anal phase, when toilet training and willful struggles with the parents normally intrude on the child in a significant way, when he is constantly beset with the prohibitions—Don't touch! Don't hit! Don't break! Don't run away!—that characterize this time known as the "terrible twos." Nowadays we generally view this period in a larger developmental context, and I have come to refer to it, only half-jokingly, as the anal-depressive-rapprochement-gender-identity phase, because in it all these developmental processes are in play and being worked through simultaneously. Often at this time one can see most clearly whether the relationship between parents and children will be based primarily on mutuality or on some variety of unilateral and overly coercive socialization.

If the child is socialized predominantly through object-related love of the parents and prohibitions are reasonably negotiated, then mutuality will tend to predominate. But if he is socialized predominantly through terror and fear of abandonment, whether openly or covertly, then his suppressed urges and needs will generally surface, often in the secretive and non–object-related ways that we call perversions, either sexual perversions or the perversions of everyday life. I believe this is true whether the child complies masochistically or is defiant and rebellious, for the compliance always cloaks rebellion just as the rebellion always conceals a secret desire to surrender. Worst of all, the child who is socialized predominantly by fear and force often has no inkling of what a mutual relationship is or how it comes about, and so he will become an adult with a distorted understanding of mutuality and love.

Let me begin by giving you two clinical examples. The first seemed neither particularly noteworthy nor perverse to the patient when he came for analysis.

This man, a dermatologist, while speaking of his adolescence and college days, once mentioned that he had played on the football teams in high school and college and was kept on varsity because, although not a very good player, he was outstanding at blocking and tackling. He loved to practice tackling and would do so for hours on end, often returning to the clubhouse bloody and bruised but strangely exhilarated. The coaches admired him for his dedication, but he himself did not quite understand why tackling thrilled him so.

I pointed out that he had recently mentioned that his mother and father were physically quite distant and that they would never kiss, hug, or even touch one another, and that ordinarily neither of them touched him. I suggested that he had spent his adolescent years violently banging into tackling dummies and other men's bodies out of some desperate longing to be touched, and particularly to be touched by his mother. He began to sob, as if some trigger point had been touched, and recounted a history of incidents ranging from sexually groping a little girl when he was three years old to repeated impromptu wrestling with a friend in high school, which had gotten him accused of homosexuality. It became clear that even his choice of dermatology as a profession was to some extent conditioned by his intense need for touching, for skin contact with another human being. This patient was also something of a Don Juan, and, although his actual sexual practices were unremarkable, his desperate need for touch and sexual contact many times a day had, in fact, led to a major distortion of loving. Although he wanted to be a caring person and needed to feel that he was giving pleasure to his partners, his insatiable need for sexualized touching led him to seductions, infidelities, and painfully ruptured relationships.

My second example is of a gay male patient, a banker whose sexual orientation was not in question but who had come for analysis because of difficulties with work and relationships. While he also felt that what he most wanted was to have a loving and enduring relationship, he constantly found himself in leather bars with one-night pickups with whom he indulged in sadomasochistic acts like licking their boots or being fist-fucked, which afterward disgusted him and made him feel loathsome. He viewed himself as a geisha girl, seducing strong men by his compliant availability but then leaving them first for fear of being abandoned. Indeed, he himself had in many ways been emotionally abandoned by a mother who throughout his childhood was distant and physically unresponsive and who eventually left the family for a lesbian relationship.

Although the dermatologist's sexual practice was usually missionary copulation, whereas the gay banker's was usually masturbation, fellatio, or anal intercourse involving actual or fantasied

humiliation and domination, it seemed to me that certain of their
dynamics were very similar and that the essence of their perversions lay, not in their sexual orientation or even their sexual practices, but in the nature of their object relationships. For although
perversion has historically meant sexual behavior that is pathological because it deviates in object choice or aim from the ostensible
norm of heterosexual genital intercourse, I am using it here in the
larger sense of an ego deficit that interferes with the adequate
resolution of object choice.

Both these accomplished men were sensitive, intelligent and
moral human beings who were struggling with all their might to
have loving and meaningful human relationships and were tortured
by their inability to do so. Both their analyses proceeded along similar lines and eventually enabled them to love in ways that felt more
satisfactory to them. But I am getting ahead of my story.

How did it happen that I saw related dynamics and a similar
evolution in these two men, one of whom was gay and practiced
anal licking and fist-fucking while the other was straight and
practiced missionary sex? Despite the apparent differences, the
similarity that seemed crucial to me was that they were both sadomasochistically fixated and that this fixation was contributing
more than anything else to their difficulties in forming loving relationships. Of course, I should differentiate these two cases, which I
view as perverse yet *organized* attempts at *establishing* object relationships, from a lower level of fragmented, indiscriminate perverse activities like subway flashing, which are basically efforts to
establish self-cohesion and may be *chaotic* attempts at *canceling* object relationships.

Freud (1919) considered the beating fantasy to be the essence
of sadomasochism, and I have related to you how I began to un-
cover the dermatologist's beating fantasy by connecting it with his
need to be touched by his mother. This need to be touched had been
transformed into a need for brutal and violent contact with other
men's bodies and connected to an unconscious fantasy of being
beaten by his father. By contrast, the gay banker's beating fantasy
was being consciously reenacted in leather bars when he got men
to abuse him, but it was also being *unconsciously* reenacted in certain repeated failures in his business life. Both men had their object relationships and their love lives structured by their beating
fantasies. How had this come about?

First let me make it clear that I believe sadomasochism, like most other psychological phenomena, is both complex and multiply determined. I have elsewhere (Bach, 1994) discussed other important factors, including endogenous temperamental factors, such as aggression in the infant, that might make it difficult or impossible for any caregiver to respond in a good enough way, thus compromising the regulation of a dyad that may then become the matrix for sadomasochism. I have also found sadomasochistic pathology to arise when the mother is endangered, sick, or unhappy and the child dedicates his life to curing or rescuing her, a frequent motif among members of our own profession. Sadomasochistic pathology often follows from a variety of childhood traumas that led to an intensification of annihilation or castration anxiety. Sadomasochism is also not uncommon in children after a prolonged illness like polio or rheumatic fever where they were isolated from their peers, afraid for their life, and in compensation created a pain-seeking and omnipotent fantasy world. Any vicissitude of life and any developmental phase may contribute to the formation of sadomasochism, but the thread that binds them all together is that relationships with primary objects become oriented predominantly toward pain rather than pleasure, so that what feels familiar, reassuring, and longed for is some variety of painful rather than pleasurable interaction. You may notice that I treat addiction to the giving or receiving of pain, that is, sadism or masochism, as two reversible sides of the same coin. In chapter 2, I made the distinction between two narcissistic types, the overinflated, grandiose, and aggressive sadist, who is defending against his weakness and vulnerability, and the deflated, helpless, and dependent masochist, who is defending against his latent grandiosity and aggression. Thus, in my experience, every sadist is a latent masochist and every masochist a potential sadist, depending on the time and the context.

Let me return to my two cases and explore one particular aspect of how this addiction to pain rather than pleasure arises. The beating fantasy in both these cases took the form of "a man is beating someone"; the gay banker had had this fantasy interpreted in a previous analysis as relating to oedipal competition with his father, who was indeed a powerful and frightening figure. Although the beating fantasy is one of Freud's (1919) great clinical discoveries, it seems likely that part of his clinical material came from the

analysis of his own daughter, and perhaps this in some way affected his ability to fully understand its consequences. At the oedipal level, where he was working with Anna, he could formulate
that the wish to be beaten by the father is "not only the punishment for the forbidden genital relation, but also the regressive substitute for that relation" (p. 189). He could then go on to conclude
that "people who harbor phantasies of this kind develop a special
sensitiveness and irritability toward anyone whom they can include in the class of fathers. They are easily offended by a person of
this kind, and in that way (to their own sorrow and cost) bring
about the realization of the imagined situation of being beaten by
their father" (p. 195), a brilliant clinical formulation as true today
as it was then.

What Freud may have overlooked, perhaps because of historical
and countertransferential difficulties, was the fantasy's preoedipal
function in maintaining the dependent tie to the father or mother
or analyst, a function I have read as, "Do anything you want to
me—beat me if you wish with whips or interpretations—but don't
ever leave me." Here the fantasy works to retain the tie to the
Mother of Pain and to avoid the establishment of newer and more
appropriate object relations. And, indeed, it seems possible that
Anna Freud's beating fantasies, despite years of analysis, may have
finally disappeared only after she had separated from her fa-
ther-analyst and found a life of her own in her relationship with
Dorothy Burlingham (Young-Bruehl, 1988).

So, among the many aspects of sadomasochism, the one that I
am emphasizing here is its origin in the tie to the caregiver and the
environmental mother. The mothers of both patients manifested a
narcissistic style of relating that I have often found in parents of
children who later develop either distorted love relationships or
outright sexual perversions. Because of the parents' self-preoccu-
pation, they can at best attend to their children only sporadically,
with an intermittent decathexis (Furman and Furman, 1984) that
undermines the child's sense of self- and object constancy. Even
worse, the basic fabric of the ego is weakened because the parent's
difficulties with cognitive and emotional self-regulation are passed
on to the child in the form of disorganized, contradictory, and in-
compatible procedural knowledge. This procedural knowledge,
which consists of abilities and rules that we learn without awareness, like the grammar of our first language, is in fact an operative

grammar of skills and procedures, including implicit goals and regulatory interactions with others, that allow us to feel that we belong in the world and know what we are doing there, just as we speak our first language without thinking about it. Because these children have internalized defective regulatory processes and procedural skills from their environment, they never feel at home in the world and always feel deviant, no matter how successful they may appear to be. Perversions of all sorts are one kind of sexualized attempt to compensate for these hidden feelings of deviance and defectiveness.

Although the parents I am discussing may often appear normal to the casual observer, they all live in a world of their own to which the child feels he has little or no access. Children learn to access their parents' cognitive and emotional states from the very beginning, and we have experimental and developmental evidence of how profoundly an infant is affected when, for example, the mother either avoids or aggressively pursues eye contact (Beebe and Stern, 1977), or when she neutralizes her own facial expression as an experimental condition (Tronick et al., 1978). If you can visualize this neutral, impassively faced experimental condition as a permanent way of relating, then you can imagine what it is like to have as your primary object a Sphinx-like caregiver whose mental and emotional experience remains a mystery to you. Obviously, the caregiver does not always have to be impassive; the effects are equally bad if she is emotionally labile, alexithymic, or in denial of her feelings. Her true feelings and thoughts remain mysterious to the child because they cannot be consistently correlated with either his own emotional states or with events in the larger world. So the child cannot understand the caregiver's mind and the caregiver remains mysterious, neither knowing the child nor being known by him. The child is confused and at a loss; he feels that the world makes no sense, he cannot orient himself in it, and he does not feel at home.

The parent's unresponsiveness, inconsistency, and unreadability is experienced by the child as a series of repeated betrayals—a cumulative trauma that undermines the stability of the self- and object representations. Questions of which mother is real intermingle in the child's mind with questions of which self is real. The child may feel constantly enraged—trapped in an environment structured by his own ambivalence, longing for a genuine relationship while struggling against a deep attachment to someone who is so emotionally unpredictable. Typically, the rage cannot be expressed and the child ends by shaming and blaming *himself* for not being able to reach the mother, whom he has idealized to protect her from his aggression.

In addition, this type of caregiver is also anhedonic; that is, she derives little or no pleasure from the parent–child relationship and ultimately provides no pleasure to the child. In most of my cases, this lack of mutual pleasure in the dyad, or even an outright sharing of suffering with the Mother of Pain, that begins in infancy and continues through each developmental stage is a prominent factor in the development of sadomasochism.

The child of such a mother is typically enraged at her, consciously or unconsciously, but cannot display his rage because she is all that he has. Such a caregiver does not allow her child any freedom, and the child clings to her because he has not been encouraged to develop his own agency. These sadomasochistic dyads are a closely coupled system without autonomy for either caregiver or child, who have indeed become each other's slaves. A normal dyad is loosely coupled; while each partner can experience togetherness, he can also experience moments of aloneness, autonomy, and effectance. Since the child cannot express his hatred *to* the caregiver and is also not obtaining any pleasure *from* her, the rage tends to become sexualized and displaced elsewhere in a perverted demand for love that reminds one of King Ludwig of Bavaria, who used to beat his subjects while shouting, "I will *make* you love me!"

This close coupling of the sadomasochistic dyad not only precludes autonomy but also effectively excludes the oedipal third, so that an illusory dyadic closeness is maintained at the expense of an entry into the real, triadic, oedipal world. In some way these children, who become our patients, are both tied to their caregivers and yet always trying to escape from them. As adults, they develop similar love–hate relationships with others in which they seem bound to the relationship through pain.

My patient, the gay banker whose beating fantasies were enacted in leather bars, was able to find a loving relationship with a man only after psychologically separating from his mother by working through the early ties that had left him addicted to painful interactions. Before that, each time he visited his mother he would afterward find himself having anonymous masochistic sex, a compensatory repetition that became clear to him only in the analysis. As a child he had desperately wanted his impassive mother and his egotistical father to respond to him in some intimate way that would confirm his existence and their relationship with him. This need led him increasingly to provocative behaviors aimed at evoking any kind of response, and the symbolic beatings that he provoked from his father were later reenacted as real beatings in leather bars.

In this chapter, I have touched on certain aspects of perversion while necessarily omitting many others. I have modified the definition of perversion from the usual "deviation in object choice or aim from heterosexual genital intercourse," which I find problematic in many ways, to the larger sense of a "deviation that interferes with the normal resolution of object choice " or "an incapacity to relate to an object as a whole person rather than as a selfobject or thing," a definition I find more relevant for psychoanalysis.

I have made some rather obvious connections, the most obvious being that, if the caregiver cannot consistently relate to the child as a whole person in a mutual relationship, then the child may have problems later in life with loving relations. These problems will often emerge as sadomasochistic character pathology with beating fantasies and regulatory difficulties that may lead to deviant sexual behaviors and sometimes to drug abuse, eating disorders, or somatic pathology.

From one perspective, all these syndromes can be viewed as disorders of self- and mutual regulation, resulting from the asynchrony between parent and child that I have described and that Ferenczi (1933) first characterized as a "confusion of tongues." But the degree of disruption may vary widely from a totally chaotic and fragmented self-organization to a relatively cohesive organization. Patients who feel quite fragmented may make desperate attempts at establishing self-cohesion and self-regulation through any and all modalities, such as filling the body with food or emptying it, altering states of consciousness by drugs or other means, altering somatic sensations in various parts of the body, or employing sexuality in a frantic attempt to revitalize the self and retain self-cohesion, as in certain sadistic sexual attacks. With all these patients there is either an acute or a cumulative environmental trauma, which they recreate and recount through enactments in the transference rather than through symbolic verbal means. In the early

part of treatment they tend to react poorly to symbolic interpretations and often experience them as a repetition of the original environmental trauma. Nevertheless, it is important eventually to
interpret internal conflicts in order to enable their sense of agency
and to help them feel responsible for their own life.

In the treatment itself, my clinical emphasis is usually on the
sadomasochistic pathology in the relationship rather than on its
symptomatic manifestations as a disorder of sexuality, of drug
abuse, or of somatization. Thus another way of thinking about perversion is as a disorder of sexual regulation, and especially of pleasure–pain regulation in the dyad. And, although neither of my
patients, the gay banker or the dermatologist, suffered from the
more primitive chaotic disorganizations, they both had enormous
problems with self-regulation. For example, they both felt incapa-
ble of being alone and were perpetually on the prowl for homosex-
ual or heterosexual contacts to make a connection, to feel alive, and
to allay their anxieties. In so doing they were both ultimately seeking to replay the original dyadic relationship with their caregivers,
but this time to get it correctly regulated. Despite countless attempts on the part of both men to work this out in real life with a
variety of partners, it was only in the psychoanalytic transference
relation that it became a genuine possibility.

In the transference, of course, we eventually expect to see some
permutation of the sadomasochistic relations that originally brought
the patient into treatment. Our hope is that, before the sadomasochism becomes explosive, we will have built up enough analytic trust
to enable the patient to talk to us about it rather than abandoning
the analysis or embroiling it in perpetual enactments. The treatment
of sadomasochism is one of our most difficult tasks, and ultimately,
as Freud noted, we must call up the ghosts in order to lay them to
rest. And while it is indeed tragic if the treatment should end in yet
another sadomasochistic impasse, of which the patient might already have had more than his share, I imagine that anyone who has
practiced long enough has at least one ending of this sort on his con-
science. A redeeming thought is that we continue to talk and theo-
rize about our clinical practice, because I believe that viewing the
therapeutic situation as a human predicament in which we are mutually engaged, and accepting responsibility for our ignorance and
our mistakes is one step on the road away from perversions in the
ongoing struggle toward stable and loving commitments.

8

TWO WAYS OF BEING

We do not know the Hells and Heavens of people we pass in the street. There are two possible perspectives. According to the first, on a minuscule ball of earth, in a smudge of mold called a city, some microorganisms move around, less durable than mayflies. And the internal states of (such) beings, deprived of any reason for their existence, perfectly interchangeable, what importance can they have? According to the second perspective, that of a reversed telescope, every one of these beings grows up to the size of a cathedral and surpasses in its complexity any nature, living or inert. Only in the second case can we see that no two persons are identical and that we may at best try to guess what is going on inside our fellow men.

—Czeslaw Milosz, *Unattainable Earth*

I suggest that there is an interface of two different ways of knowing or thinking or of being in the world that is pervasive in human

107

life. I trust that this will not remain a purely poetic or philosophical notion, because in the end I hope to illustrate its clinical importance and show how we struggle in every analytic hour with the difficulties it presents.

These two states of consciousness or two ways of perceiving or being in the world are familiar to everyone, but perhaps under very different names or categories. I am talking about what has been referred to as the opposition of the Apollonian and the Dionysian, or the Classical and the Romantic; but it could equally well be seen as the contrast between the tragic and the enthusiastic, or between pessimistic and optimistic outlooks, or between the obsessive and the hysterical approach, or even between secondary process and primary process.

One could point to the distinction that Winnicott makes between Doing and Being or, at the risk of being politically incorrect, it might be articulated as the difference between masculine and feminine. In physics, it might be seen in the contradiction between Einstein's model of determinate objectivity and Bohr's (1963) model of complementarity; in philosophy, one might compare the correspondence theory of truth with the coherence theory of truth; in theology or religious practice, one might think of the separation of the profane and the sacred; in poetics or literature, one might recall Coleridge's discrimination between the primary and the secondary imagination; and, in sociology, one might think of Foucault's distinction between cognition and experience. The list could be extended indefinitely, because similar dichotomies can be found in almost every field of human endeavor, but I suggest that all these contrasting points of view are complex transformations of our two primary states of consciousness: subjectivity and objectivity.

What I am calling subjective awareness is a state in which we are totally into ourselves and our feelings with the rest of the world as background, that is, something akin to a Romantic or Dionysian state of mind, and in certain respects analogous to Rousseau's noble savage. This was presumed to be the original conscious state of the neonate, but the baby watchers tell us that within 24 hours an infant can discriminate its mother's odor, so that precursors of objective awareness begin to emerge very early. Still, objective self-awareness is usually dated from the ability to recognize oneself in the mirror, at one and a half to two years of age. Self-recognition is the precursor of self-reflection, the ability to view oneself objectively from the outside as if looking at another person, that is, the Classical or Apollonian state of mind. I need hardly remind you that in psychoanalysis we expend an enormous amount of effort trying to help our patients reflect on themselves and become able to entertain a state of objective or reflective self-awareness, and that the success or failure of the treatment often depends on their being able to do this.

You may remember the young woman who, complaining of her inability to have a mutual orgasm with her lover, said, "I can't make the smooth transition. . . . I'm either *me*, totally me and so excited that nothing else exists, or else I'm Tony's lover, and I can give him pleasure, but then I don't have it myself." When she was totally involved in her own sexual excitement, she was in a state of subjective awareness; when she was Tony's lover, she was objectively aware of herself, observing herself from the outside, as if she were standing on the ceiling or on Mars and watching herself in the world.

I have some recorded observations, written in a baby book by the mother of a patient when he was seven years old. When in a state of subjective awareness he once said, "This world terrifies me sometimes. . . . It seems to be all me!" He was afraid that his subjectivity, overburdened with narcissistic grandiosity, had encompassed everything, leaving him feeling as if he pervaded the entire world, and yet he was simultaneously terrified of being all alone. Conversely, when in a state of objective self-awareness he once asked, "Is this world a *dreaming* or is it real?" expressing his sense of himself as standing outside his experience and observing it as if it were a dream, as if it were happening to someone else. Already at age seven he was disturbed by both his subjectivity and his objectivity because they seemed unintegrated, uncontrolled, and unrelated to other human beings, just as he felt emotionally unrelated to his mother.

Of course, most of us oscillate between these two states; at times we are un–self-consciously lost in what we are doing, and at other times we are very aware of ourselves as if we were viewing ourselves from the outside as others might see us. So, in effect, we are all both Dionysians and Apollonians, Romantics and Classicists, but a crucial difference lies in our preferred mode of being and also in our abilities to transition or oscillate flexibly and appropriately between these states. Another important difference lies in the degree to which these two states have been integrated or assimilated. In pathology they are radically opposed—"I'm either all me, or else I'm someone else's object"—whereas ordinarily we can be in a subjective state, centered on ourselves and yet, through interpenetration, still experience ourselves as participants in the larger world. We have to remember that the grandiose self or object and the mirroring self or object (Kohut, 1971), while extremely valuable clinical concepts, were derived from pathology and that their analogues in normal life may be far more subtle and complexly integrated states.

But, if you will allow me a bit of poetic leeway, I could say that hysterics, extroverts, and acting-outers tend to prefer the Romantic mode of being; that is, they are in unreflective communion with their nature and doing their own thing without taking too much perspective on their actions. In this way they resemble the Romantic writers and poets who disdained and outraged social conventions, sought ecstasy in drugs, and were ready, in Baudelaire's language, to voyage "anywhere out of this world." On the other hand, obsessives, introverts, and schizoid types prefer the Classical mode in which they reflect on their own thoughts and actions, are likely to appreciate and conform to social conventions, and seek their pleasure in more meditative and, perhaps, more durable pursuits rather than in the throes of ecstasy. In these ways, they resemble the Enlightenment thinkers and writers who, setting much store on calm and measured objectivity, valued cognition and the intellect above experience and the emotions. Thus subjectivity has been more highly valued in such periods as the Romantic era and by more hysterically oriented types, whereas objectivity has been more highly prized in such periods as the Classical era or Enlightenment and by more obsessively oriented types.

Of course, married couples often are complementary, so that the predominantly subjective disposition of one and the predominantly objective disposition of the other may offset each other. In this way, the couple can both self-regulate and have a built-in other from which each can distinguish himself or herself. We can easily think of friends, relatives, and even colleagues who fall into one camp or the other, but for most of us our own regulatory processes are sufficiently integrated, we hope, that most of the time we make the transition between subjectivity and objectivity in a way that is more or less appropriate to the task at hand.

Unfortunately, there are many who cannot do so—and this brings us to the realm of psychopathology. A good analytic patient, for example, is expected to be able to free-associate, that is, to enter a state of subjective awareness and eventually to make the transition to objective self-awareness by pausing to reflect on his free associations. Even the best of analytic patients will occasionally be unable to associate subjectively or else be unable to reflect objectively on his associations for dynamic reasons, which can then be analyzed. But our more disturbed patients may hardly ever be able to free-associate, either because they cannot enter a state of subjective awareness or because they cannot verbalize it. Others may hardly ever be able to reflect on their associations, either because they are unable to view themselves objectively or because it is unbearably shameful for them to share their reflections with someone else. Indeed, it may take years before some patients can trust us enough to free-associate, and even more years before they can allow themselves or us to make objective comments about these associations.

The pathology that we are dealing with involves homeostasis, the regulation of these two states of consciousness and their dialectic. For example, in chapter 2, I distinguish two kinds of narcissistic patients: the inflated sadistic type, who presents with open grandiosity and an unconscious sense of worthlessness, and the deflated masochistic type, who presents with open feelings of worthlessness and an unconscious sense of grandiosity. The inflated type exists primarily in a state of subjectivity, concerned only with himself, and unable to be objective about his aspirations, but unconsciously he feels worthless and self-critical. The deflated type exists primarily in a state of objective self-awareness, masochistically denigrating and criticizing himself as if he were some hostile outside observer, but unconsciously he may feel quite special or grandiose.

In both cases the smooth continuum of states of consciousness is sharply split or dichotomized, and neither type is able to transition flexibly between viewing himself subjectively and viewing himself objectively, as we normally do. Their difficulties with emotional control are also connected to this pathology of regulation; unable to make smooth transitions, they flip back and forth between Apollonian and Dionysian affect states, between overinhibition and overexcitement. Whichever state they find themselves in can be frightening because they feel helpless to regulate the transitions. Extreme forms of this pathology can be found in persons with manic-depressive disorders and especially in those with multiple personality disorders, for whom all attempts to integrate the subjective and the objective in the same self have been definitively abandoned. I have suggested that all disorders of self-regulation are also disorders of subjective and objective awareness and of the somatic processes in which they are embedded. But before I proceed with this line of thought, let me present some clinical material.

Some years ago, a woman painter named Julia, with whom I had never discussed the subject, began an analytic session by saying,

J: I've just begun to see very clearly that I switch back and forth between two perspectives on myself, or two ways of looking at things. And the way that I look at what's happening seems almost more important than what's actually happening. In the first way, which I'll call column A, I have an absolute belief that the importance of living lies in using my creative juices in whatever way I can . . . that's what living is about. I don't have to figure out why it is. It just feels that way, and it doesn't matter what the outcome is 'cause the important thing is the act of doing it, the creation or nurturing of it. The important thing is just to paint, and I believe that. But when I switch to column B, I don't believe it, and I don't believe the importance of it, and it's only significant if it has a meaning for somebody else. I have to know that it has a meaning for somebody else in contrast to column A.
T: What about column B?
J: It's a sort of reflection of how I grew up in a totally communal life where nothing that I did was confirmed or appreciated and what was valuable was what other people valued . . . and it's always a problem for me because I may look at something I paint and think it's quite good, but then it always feels solipsistic and arrogant to feel that way.

In the next hour, Julia continued along the same lines and mentioned that the switches from column A to column B occur so abruptly, uncontrollably, and unpredictably in her mind that, when she is in one state, she can hardly imagine that the other state exists.

T: Does anything come to mind about these abrupt switches?
J: [After a long time] I hadn't thought of this in many years, but when I was a little girl my father used to tell me stories about all

the places we would travel to. . . . We could go to France and he would draw pictures of the bridges over the river and the Eiffel Tower, how we would sit in the café and drink hot chocolate and watch the people and the organ grinders with their monkeys. . . . I was transported, and I would sit there drinking all this in and then ask, When are we going? And he would answer that he couldn't say exactly when we were going, but that we would go sometime. . . . It was only much later that I slowly realized we weren't going anyplace, that we would never go anywhere. . . . I can't remember the actual effect that it had on me at the time. But it's the same effect now—an idea comes to me, and I think it through, and I'm going to do it, and I love it, and then comes the darkness. . . . Not that it won't happen, but that it won't go anywhere . . . just be what it was . . . that moment of excitement and anticipation and those mental images . . . that had a profound effect on me actually.

T: That's what triggers the switch from column A to column B!

J: Yes . . . it's all fantasy and imagination . . . like in the room where my father took me and spun these images, and I was completely enthralled, and then he'd say it was time to go, and the door would close, and that was okay for him, but for me it was a terrible disillusionment because the evocation was so powerful. . . . It's an abrupt switch between A and B, but my father often switched like that, and so did my mother. . . . It was confusing to me when I remembered this other stuff, because most of the time my father was totally disinterested in me, didn't know I existed, and he let my mother beat me and abuse me every single day. . . . Maybe if I could find a way, I could bring him back into column A . . . how could I feel that he was a cold, indifferent, and distant man when he was sharing this beautiful world with me?

If we consider that these incidents all took place in an immigrant family living in near-poverty in the Chicago slums, we can imagine how heartbreaking it was for this little girl to be cast from the very heights of Romantic illusion to the depths of Classical tragedy: how painful and sudden and abrupt the transition from the participatory subjective awareness of her mutual fantasies with her father to the realization of the coldly objective facts—that she had been duped, that he was indifferent to her, and that it had all been nothing but fantasy.

Later Julia described the physical manifestations of this abrupt shift from one state of consciousness to another:

J: It's all very visceral. . . . When I'm in column A, I feel it in my body like waves. . . . It's a joyous state like a warmth, a surge. It comes from the bottom of my being. And when I'm in column B, it's not like waves—it's like claws that grip me, and when they grip there's a nauseous feeling like I'm screaming from the impact of the feeling. . . . Column A is like music . . .
T: And B?
J: It's like cruelty and chills and tears come to my eyes.

I have connected the roots of what Julia called column A (i.e., subjective awareness, with the extreme excitement of the practicing period and the hyperarousal of the sympathetic nervous system) and the origins of what she called column B (i.e., objective self-awareness, with the low-keyedness or mild depression of the rapprochement child and the activation of the parasympathetic or inhibitory system). Listening to her father's stories, she is in a state of subjective awareness and hyperarousal of the sympathetic system, manifested by waves of joyous warmth and sexuality and a surge of good feelings about herself and her objects. The sudden realization that this is all an illusion abruptly terminates sympathetic arousal, cuts short these good feelings, and instantly triggers the onset of inhibitory parasympathetic tone, bringing with it bad feelings, like claws that grip, and the nausea that is characteristic of sudden parasympathetic tonus. When these alternations occur abruptly and frequently enough, they become a cumulative trauma, so that joyful arousal carries with it the threat of a precipitous fall into despair. And we now have learned (Schore, 1994) that, in response to repeated traumas of this kind, the autonomic and limbic systems become modified in such a way as to increase the probability that such shifts will be experienced as abrupt, extreme, and out of control.

Of course, we cannot hope to remain in a permanent state of joyful arousal or euphoria like the Lotus Eaters, for it is our destiny to shift between happiness and sadness, between arousal and inhibition, between the world of joyful subjectivity and the world of objective assessment of our subjectivity, between fantasy and reality. What was traumatic for Julia was not that her father had told her romantic fairy tales that would never be realized, but, rather, the abrupt disconnection between this world of fantasy and the harsh world of her everyday reality, two worlds between which there was no bridge or transitional space. One might wonder, though, if these fantasies nevertheless nourished some positive force in her creative life as a painter.

Let me contrast Julia's case with a more normal everyday incident, a charming story recently told me by a mother whose five-year-old daughter demanded to know if there really was a Tooth Fairy. She would not be put off by evasions. The mother finally admitted that the Tooth Fairy was only a story invented by adults, and her daughter seemed satisfied with this explanation. This little girl had recently experienced the death of a grandparent but seemed to be tolerating this loss in a relatively unremarkable way. Yet for the three nights following this discussion about the Tooth Fairy, she was unable to sleep well and expressed fears that she might die and that her mother would not live forever. When the mother explained that we live on in our children, the little girl was worried that she might not be able to have children of her own.

This very sophisticated mother had the distinct impression that, in addition to the grandmother's death, the Tooth Fairy was somehow involved in all this and that her husband would have handled their daughter's question about the Tooth Fairy in a better way. When I asked her how her husband might have handled it, she said without hesitation, "Oh! He would have answered, 'Of course there's a Tooth Fairy!' but with a big smile that would have left plenty of room for ambiguity. I suppose that this must be a reaction to some loss of illusion or faith, the first doubt that things aren't necessarily permanent or continuous or replaceable."

Whether one prefers the mother's method of handling this incident or the father's, what is important is the care and concern that each parent showed in handling what for this little girl was a very important part of her mourning and of the transition between illusion and disillusion and between subjectivity and objectivity.

In self-pathology we are dealing with the dialectical problem between subjective and objective self-awareness, and in those two examples we can contrast the responses of loving parents, different as they might be, with the response of a parent who showed no concern and no ability to help his child grapple with these issues. We see that normally there is a slow process of disillusionment that occurs preferably at the child's own pace. Objectivity and reality enter into the child's subjective world in a relatively nontraumatic way, so that the Tooth Fairy, for example, comes to populate a transitional world that forms the fabric of our ego and allows us to use the thought that we may perhaps live on in our children to face the brutal objective fact that we are now alive but will eventually be dead. But reality also involves the loss of illusion, and that loss always results in some depression or inhibition of affective arousal.

Mahler, as well as Klein and others, considered depression as a developmental achievement because it is only by reaching this stage of separation-individuation that the child is able to view himself from the outside, in objective self-awareness, as another person would see him. Characteristically, he finds this a sobering and somewhat depressing experience because it illuminates his own dependence and insignificance. While, in the first year of life, infants typically respond to their mirror image with unrestrained joy and enthusiasm, they start to withdraw as soon as they begin to recognize themselves in the mirror, and they become wary and self-conscious in the presence of their reflection.

Interestingly, there is often a phase of a few months after self-recognition when little Johnny points to himself and calls himself "me" but continues to point to and call his mirror image "Johnny." Looking through this little window in time, I imagine the child has realized that, for others, "Johnny" and "me" refer to the same thing, but that he himself is not quite ready to integrate his subjective, somatic awareness of himself with its invariant transformation as seen by an objective observer in the mirror.

This initial hesitation and perhaps disappointment at the transformation of the "me" into "Johnny" continues to some degree throughout life, as evidenced by the common observation that many people are shocked and disappointed by photographs or tape recordings of themselves, as well as by prolonged self-observations in a three-way mirror. We seem to have stumbled on some basic ontological gap in the world, because "me" feels very real and undeniably alive in our flesh, whereas Johnny-in-the-mirror or the other is always more a mental construction and a stranger. "Me" feels like a "who" with whom we are intimately, proprioceptively acquainted, whereas Johnny-in-the-mirror and other people feel more like a "what," whose existence we have cognitively recognized but can never quite apprehend with the same inner certainty.

I hope that by now I have given you a sense of the dichotomy between states of excited, subjective, bodily awareness, for which the developmental model is the practicing child, and states of inhibited, objective, more cognitive self-awareness, as typically seen emerging in the rapprochement child. I have also, in a far-ranging leap of speculative play, related this dichotomy to the many dichotomies that have so often engaged people in pitched battles, such as Classical versus Romantic or Apollonian versus Dionysian, correspondence theory versus coherence theory, and, in our own field, conflict versus deficit, science versus hermeneutics, and so forth. I have suggested that from one perspective these may all be related to complex derivatives of the basic states of subjectivity and objectivity. And I have implied that, just as we oscillate between subjective and objective awareness, with some inclined more in one direction and some more in the other, we may also view different conflicts, cultures and periods of history in a similar way.

But let me now descend from this grand overview and return to its developmental origins, as I understand them (Bach, 1985, 1994). We remember that the height of subjective awareness is reached in practicing and that rapprochement is characterized by a developing objective perspective on the self and, in the process, by oscillations between subjectivity and objectivity, between centering on the self and centering on the other, and between elation and despair, the "terrible twos." In psychopathology, a fixation or regression to this phase is characterized by sadomasochistic interactions between an omnipotent, sadistic, and idealized self and a masochistic and denigrated other, or vice versa.

Normally, it is the caregiver who helps the child regulate between the extremes of elation and despair, between self and other, and between the subjective and objective states of consciousness. But what occurs as the child matures is not just better regulated and more appropriate oscillations between subjectivity and objectivity or between self and other. Rather, we find a more complex synthesis involving richer levels of integration, a blending and interpenetration of the two in the transitional area so that they are no longer simply dichotomous. Thus the infant experiences the mother thinking and feeling about him, and then the mother experiences the infant experiencing her, which the infant, in turn, reexperiences. Through projection and introjection, subjectivity and objectivity become infiltrated and informed by each other; the inner world becomes penetrated and suffused by the outer world and the outer world, in its turn, becomes permeated by the inner world. Opposing qualities become integrated into a higher unity, and relatively simple states of consciousness are continually reorganized into increasingly more complex networks of interactive states that feed back into each other. The present is continuously interacting with the past, and the past is continually being retranscribed onto the present.

You will recall that, in Winnicott's (1953) original description, the transitional object, such as a piece of blanket, is literally permeated and suffused with the handling and odor of both mother and child. Thus at one and the same time it provides both a safe haven of attachment to the object and a means of separation from that very object. It is both a link to the past as it was and a way of carrying and transforming this past into the emerging future. It is a way of remaining immersed in subjectivity while also being a path toward objectifying the world, as the transitional object expands into the world of culture while at the same time losing its magical qualities so that in time it becomes simply a torn piece of blanket.

It is only when this does not occur, as in pathology, that one finds a radical splitting and an obsessive alternation between the frozen dichotomies of subjectivity and objectivity, of self and other, which seem unable to oscillate fluidly, to integrate, or to reach some homeostasis. The subjectivity of the manic or narcissistic patient differs from normal subjectivity not only quantitatively, in its extravagant intensity and unregulated swings between extremes, but also qualitatively in not being permeated with otherness, that is, in not having reached a higher level of integration of self- and object representation. Reaching these more complex levels of synthesis changes the nature of dichotomies, diminishes splitting, and, at each successive level, changes our vision of and relationship to the world. Let me now give you an example of how dichotomies are transformed at higher levels of integration and how thought processes and states of consciousness become more complex in the process.

In chapter 2, I told about a woman with multiple personality disorder who, when she was in a suicidal state, was cut off from the living experience that she was a mother who loved her children and would therefore not want to abandon them. As the treatment progressed and her self-representations became more consolidated and permeated with important object relationships by way of the transference, her subjectivity enlarged and her children also became included in her normal sphere of narcissistic omnipotence. Hers is a simple example of what I mean by the self-representation's becoming suffused and permeated with important object representations and being raised to a new level of integration so that what the patient called "forgetting" was no longer possible for her. Of course, this was far from being an unmixed blessing for her, and for a long time she was furious with me because of the many losses and deprivations that this process of self-integration entailed.

What is at issue here, of course, is not just a simple shift from subjective to objective self-awareness, because, even when suicidal, she was always able, if reminded, to make this shift to the objective and realize that she was in fact a mother with young children. But, when she was suicidal, this fact simply did not *mean* anything to her or was immediately forgotten—and this was true for her until the enlargement of her subjectivity included her children within the sphere of her normal narcissistic omnipotence. What we saw was a movement from splitting to integration, a change in her ability to make the transition between subjective and objective awareness, and also an advance in the organization of her representational processes—two of the more important factors in a complex state of consciousness.

We can find a similar progression in the following vignette from the analysis of a young man who was raised by a disturbed mother. One of his most traumatic memories was of a night alone with his mother when she became quite psychotic and insisted that the house was on fire. When he came for analysis, he was unable to maintain an objective view of his mother and would either fall completely under her spell or else be obliged to escape physically in order to view her objectively. After some years of analysis, he dreamed that he and his twin were struggling for their mother's attention. After various competitive maneuvers, he suddenly said to his twin, "This is absurd!" and they embraced and walked off together holding hands, leaving their mother behind. That was one of the earliest indications of consolidating self-representations and a beginning separation from his mother.

A few days later, he had the following dream:

It's about my mother. . . . She told me the house is on fire, and I looked, and it is! She said, see, it's burning, and I couldn't believe it, but it was true, and then I looked again, and I saw that it wasn't true.

There are two realities. . . . There's the feeling of being swept up in what's going on with my mother . . . I want so much to be close to her, and it's impossible . . . part of me believing what my mother tells me . . . that's the first time I actually dreamed about that memory, when I was a little boy . . . one of my scariest memories . . . unacknowledged by her, she doesn't remember anything of it, it's all gone . . . I didn't expect her to remember it. . . . Everything she was doing was weird and crazy.

One of my biggest fears is that she tells me something, and it's true. . . . The scary thing is that she's right . . . the worst thing that comes to mind is, maybe it's not them, it's me! In the dream of the twins, one believes and the other one doesn't believe my mother. . . . I can't work this through with my mother because she doesn't remember anything.

A week later he had another dream:

I let my dog out of the house, and he died. . . . He was running around, crashing into walls, and finally just collapsed. . . . There was a horrifying moment when I picked him up, and I thought he was dead, but then I looked again, and he was okay, and he started to walk around again.

His associations:

After my disappointment about not getting the job, I wanted to call my girlfriend and be with her, but we had been fighting, so I went home and went to bed by myself and had this dream about the dog. . . . All of these dreams I had . . . it's still new for me to feel different things at the same time. . . . It used to be that if I focused on one thing, then another thing would get blocked out and pushed away. . . . It's a very new experience for me . . . something that's definitely changed . . . .I can do more than one thing at a time . . . I can feel upset about something and still manage to get pleasure out of something

else . . . I know that today I feel sad, but that doesn't blot out
the other things that I've been feeling. . . . I'm so used to
things being black and white in my family . . . that's the way
we always operated . . . so I'm uncomfortable with this because it's still new . . . but I'm beginning to see that it's okay to
miss my girlfriend and feel sad about it but still feel angry at
her and not have to go back to her. . . . It feels weird.

What he is describing is that he no longer feels engulfed by his
subjectivity but has become able to sustain an objective point of
view and to make more appropriate transitions between subjectivity and objectivity. Furthermore, he is able to encompass these
multiple points of view and contrary affects within an enlarged
self-representation that is part of an emergent and more complex
state of consciousness. One might say that he is beginning to create
a psychic space within which his subjective experiences of himself
and his experiences of himself as seen by others are beginning to
coalesce. In terms of our mirror analogy, "Johnny" and "me" are
beginning to feel more like the same person, a person who has an
ongoing continuity of being across diverse times, places, and states
of consciousness.

Let me conclude by turning once more from a microanalysis of
self-representations to the macroanalysis of a level of cultural representation and try to show how analogous forces are at work here
too. I had planned to conclude this chapter with some recent literary research demonstrating that the 18th century, so renowned for
its rationality and objectivity, also in a certain sense "invented the
uncanny. Thus, the very psychic and cultural transformations that
led to the . . . glorification of that period as an age of reason or enlightenment . . . also produced, like a kind of toxic side effect, a new
human experience of strangeness, anxiety, bafflement and intellectual impasse" (Castle, 1995, p. 8). I saw this view as illustrating
my thesis that extreme cultural objectivity seems to create the
conditions for a reversion to subjectivity, and vice versa.

But just as I had finished writing, I came across this half-page arti-
cle in the *New York Times*, which I cite in somewhat condensed form:

Paris, April 29, 1996
The French see themselves as a people who appreciate method
and logic. Their teenagers are taught logic and philosophy

in school. Intricate discourse fills as much television time as any national sport. And this year the country is making a fuss over Rene Descartes, France's emblem of rational thought, who was born 400 years ago.

Yet a contradiction arises that the great philosopher himself might have liked to consider: Why are the French spending so much time these days with psychics and seers?

A recent poll showed that more French men and women believe in the devil today than a decade ago. The French are reportedly consulting clairvoyants and numerologists in greater numbers than ever. Demand is also up for people who seek underground water with a dowsing rod, heal the sick by telephone and interpret handwriting.

"It's bizarre, but it's very clear that the more machines we build, the less we know how to live and the more we are all searching," said Ange d'Orment, a psychic.

The Government has evidence that magic is thriving. Last year, the tax authorities said that close to 50,000 taxpayers, the highest number ever, had declared income from their work as stargazers, healers, mediums and similar occupations. By comparison, the country had fewer than 36,000 Roman Catholic priests and some 6000 psychiatrists. . . .

Some say all this activity shows the great fear of the end of the millennium. Others see it as a result of the erosion of other systems like institutional religion, Marxist ideology and psychoanalysis.

"My clients think that psychoanalysis is very exotic," said Alain Beunard, a self-styled druid who keeps a discreet office above the Paris wax museum. The place was hard to find, he explained, because his clients—"businessmen, politicians and so on"—do not like to be seen there.

"We've become too scientific, too intellectual," Mr. Beunard said. "People want something direct, something simple."

My understanding is that every turn toward objectivity carries within it the seeds of a reversion to subjectivity and vice versa. Although we might hope that each reversion will lead to some higher level of integration, this is unfortunately not always the case.

Progression to higher levels of synthesis is difficult to achieve and is always bought at something of a price. My suicidal patient had, by incorporating her children into her subjectivity, become more firmly anchored in reality, but at the cost of giving hostages to fortune. Moreover, she sometimes experienced her ensuing inability to commit suicide as an unpleasant constraint and a loss of freedom.

I imagine it is a loss in some ways that men in our Western culture are no longer able to achieve the cosmic state of consciousness that must have been the everyday experience of the Paleolithic hunter, for whom an animal was a miraculous totem and the hunt a sacred encounter between the ecstatic, endangered hunter and the awesome, terrifying manifestation of the animal-god. Primitive yearnings from that time may still surface in a degenerate way in the rituals of the bullfight; in the annual hunting seasons when bearded men in totemic costumes roam the woods to slaughter deer with their weapons; or perhaps even in certain seemingly inexplicable atrocities and wars.

I have tried to sketch a sweeping overview of one aspect of psychic change and development as it emerges on the level of the individual and on the level of culture. On either level, it always seems difficult for us to pay the price of loss and mourning, to abandon a familiar dichotomy for the uncertainty of arriving at a deeper integration. I hope, nevertheless, that I have encouraged you in our ongoing efforts to do just that.

9

PSYCHOANALYSIS AND LOVE

In a famous 1906 letter to Carl Jung, Freud wrote, "The [psychoanalytic] cure is effected by love" (McGuire, 1974, pp. 12–13). A little more than a month later, at a meeting of the Vienna Psychoanalytic Society, he again commented, "Our cures are cures of love" (Nunberg and Federn, 1962, p. 101). Indeed, Freud once told a colleague, Max Eitingon, that the "secret of therapy is to cure through love" (Grotjahn, 1967, p. 445).

And yet, as I glance through the catalogs of our psychoanalytic institutes, out of hundreds of courses I could find not one devoted to love and only one with the word love in the title. I am reminded of the old joke about a young fellow with a broken watch who passed a store from which a large model of a watch was hanging. When he walked in to get his watch repaired, the old man behind the counter explained that he did not repair watches, that he was in fact a *mohel*, a person who performs ritual circumcisions. When the young fellow angrily asked him why he had a large watch hanging outside, the old man replied, "And what else should I hang outside?"

Analogously, there seems to be reluctance on the part of psychoanalysts to display love as the model for what it is that they repair, which, of course, is perfectly understandable from many points of view. No doubt were I to ask the dean at any of these institutes why there are no courses on the nature of love, he might answer, "How can we teach a course on love? This is a school for mental health professionals where we teach psychoanalytic technique and how to treat mental health problems. We expect that issues of loving will be dealt with in one's training analysis!"

And he would be right. When we teach the usual courses on technique, we are placing the emphasis on the agency of the psychoanalyst; that would no doubt be the appropriate way to teach a technical procedure in medicine, computer science, or shoe repair. But perhaps we should be placing the emphasis, not on the doctor and his technique, but on the patient and the patient's sense of agency and empowerment. There may be a vital difference in whether we relate to our patients primarily through psychoanalytic technique or primarily through love. Perhaps love and psychoanalytic technique do not inhabit the same realm of discourse. For one may teach and sometimes even learn psychoanalytic technique, but love is an act of grace for which one can only prepare.

Love is a difficult subject for everyone, and for psychoanalysts it is fraught with problems of transference and countertransference, the weight of social attitudes and collegial judgments, special ethical considerations, and even legal concerns. Perhaps that is why psychoanalysts, following in Freud's shadow, have so often chosen to deal with love as a technical issue rather than attempting to face love as the controlling force implied in Freud's statement, "The secret of therapy is to cure by love." Many of the technical terms and concepts of psychoanalysis can be seen as part of a programmatic effort to specify the parameters of love in an experience-distant language. This technical language has both advantages and disadvantages: while it may give us some perspective on our emotions by allowing us to think about them symbolically and to discuss them with colleagues and patients, it also tends to deprive our words of life and leaves us with a hollow discourse about the technicalities of loving without the essence of the thing itself.

I mention this dilemma to show what a vexing topic love is and how complicated and perplexing our ideas and attitudes about love have been and still remain. Freud (1915a) did write one paper, "Observations on Transference Love," as part of a series on the technique of psychoanalysis. But here again his emphasis was on the technical management of the explosive and embarrassing situation in which a woman patient might precipitously declare her love for her male analyst. Freud certainly knew about this situation from personal experience. He was clear that the analyst should not return the patient's love, by which he meant that the analyst cannot have sex with the patient; on the other hand, the analyst must *not* encourage the patient to repress those feelings because they are central to the patient's erotic life and must be relived. Freud advised us to show the patient that her love is not real love but only a transferred or transference love, because of its function as a resistance and also because it is composed almost entirely of archaic love elements from past relationships. But then, in a moment of inspired doubt, he wondered with us if this transference love is in fact really any different from genuine love, which, in his own words, is also "more similar to abnormal than to normal mental phenomena" (p. 168). It seems that he was never able to resolve this quandary to his own lasting satisfaction. We might note here Freud's (1915) occasional view of love as a pathological phenomenon, as well as the difficulties he had discussing the analyst's feelings of love apart from their expression in sexual relations.

And, indeed, particularly in those bygone days when psychoanalysis was experiencing a wave of popularity, one frequently heard people say that they would never go into analysis because they did not want to fall in love with their analyst. Now, of course, we know that not everyone who goes into psychoanalysis falls in love with his analyst, just as not everyone who goes into church falls in love with God. In fact, many people, in one way or another, are unable to love and this may be the very reason that brings them into analysis.

There was a time when we heard a great deal about "women who loved too much," women who repeatedly fell head over heels in love with men who cruelly mistreated them, and the popular opinion was that women loved too much and most men did not love enough. Analysis of these cases revealed that there was more than a quantitative factor involved and that some women who seemed to love too much really could not love enough in the right sort of way. And the same applied to men.

One might think that the psychoanalytic situation would be a perfect setting for helping us deepen our understanding about love: here we have two human beings intimately involved with each other in ways that predispose to love and who have also vowed to be completely honest with each other and not to act out love sexually. The analytic setting does, in fact, constitute an ideal love laboratory, but unfortunately the passions aroused by love have all too often interfered with the objective collection of data. We have seen that even Freud (1915), the very inventor of this love laboratory, was tempted to abandon the entire project when a pretty young patient threw herself into his recently married arms, and even years later how he tries to manage a similar situation by telling his patient that her transference love is not real, all the while wondering, with his characteristic honesty and intellectual rigor, whether or not he is telling her the truth.

Whether we are watching Freud (1915a) struggle with his dis-covery of the erotic transference or follow Ferenczi (1988) as he tries to love his patients better than a good mother would, we are witnessing the analyst wrestling with insults to his narcissism and the disturbance of his narcissistic balance by the tensions provoked in the analytic situation. And these men were, after all, the best love researchers we had! Freud and Ferenczi each had a very differ-ent kind of tolerance for disturbances of their narcissistic equilib-rium, and this difference was one factor that allowed each of them to make their distinctive discoveries. Others, with fewer scruples, simply abandoned themselves to their passions or used the pa-tients for their own satisfactions in more devious and reprehensi-ble ways. As we think about it, we become aware that the powers of the Goddess of Love reach not only to the most sublime of human experience but also to the most degraded.

This thought brings to mind the multifarious so-called perver-sions of love that have existed since time immemorial. I still re-member my consternation the first time I met a patient who told me with great embarrassment that his love object was a carefully preserved rubber raincoat. I recall, too, the mixture of emotions that engulfed me as I first heard the intimate, detailed descriptions of tortures, beatings, mutilations, and other S&M practices that people inflict on each other by mutual consent. It took a great deal of time and self-reflection to work through my initial reactions of fear, horror, loathing, fascination, and shifting identifications before I was able to arrive at a place where I could actually listen to what was being told me and try to understand what it meant. The people who engaged in these practices were sometimes people you might *not* want to have as friends, but often enough they were people of the highest moral and cultural standards, people you *might* want to have as friends, people who were tortured by their secret obsessions and their self-loathing. It was only slowly that I began to understand that all of us are really looking for the same thing and that, for reasons that could be uncovered by psychoanalysis, people with perversions have simply strayed onto a false path or taken a wrong turn in their search for the road leading to love. It proved to be a not impossible task to retrace these steps and help many of these people find the path that was right for them, and this success was very gratifying indeed.

But it also taught me that a key issue in doing successful psychoanalysis is how to enter into the experiential world of the patient, the world in which the patient is living—that is, to enter into the patient's psychic reality, which requires leaving behind, as far as possible, one's own fears, memories, values, and desires. Now, that is a tall order under any circumstances, and it seemed particularly difficult to abandon my own desires and values to empathize with someone for whom loving meant pouring hot wax on someone's genitals till they screamed in pain, or for whom being loved meant being fist-fucked or screaming in pain. Sometimes I would find myself knowing how I was supposed to be listening but not really being able to listen, or sometimes I would feel that I was the one being psychically tortured by the patient and was unable to put away my natural reactions and recover my narcissistic equilibrium. But I learned that the important thing was to keep trying, even if I could not always succeed.

My friend Irving Steingart (1995) has written some moving words about how an analyst must learn to love the patient's psychic reality, and I agree with him that in a good analysis the analyst is constantly working toward understanding, and indeed toward loving, his patient's psychic reality.

I would add that in my own experience the patient also comes to understand and love the analyst's psychic reality and that this is part of my definition of what true love is all about. In a good analysis the analyst comes to love the patient's psychic reality including her whole embodied reality. Love in the sense of knowing, appreciating, and admiring without carnal knowledge or seductive feelings but in essentially the same way one appreciates the body and flesh of one's closest friends or one's own children in their entirety.

This reminds me of one of the first patients I ever treated, about 50 years ago, whom I will call Mrs. Brown. I was a young student when, as my first case at a large clinic, Mrs. Brown was referred to me with the diagnosis of paranoid schizophrenia. When I met her I found a chronically depressed young woman who weighed close to 300 pounds. She had dropped out of high school, was the mother of two children, and was married to a man who also sounded schizophrenic. I was young and foolish and began the treatment with high hopes—despite the cynicism and cautions of my supervisor. I soon noticed that Mrs. Brown was very intelligent and, perhaps because of this, her attitude toward the treatment seemed as cynical and cautious as my supervisor's. Not much seemed to happen as we slowly got to know each other, and after almost a year had gone by I was still very much engaged but becoming less hopeful. Then one day as I walked into the office with Mrs. Brown and watched her settle in, I did not even notice her weight and I found myself thinking how beautiful she was, as if I were seeing her for the first time. As I now understand in retrospect, from that moment on things began to take off in a most unusual way. Mrs. Brown decided to go back to school. She finished her equivalency, went on to college and then later to graduate school. Along the way she shed her excess weight and divorced her husband. When I last heard, she had moved, remarried, and was teaching at a university out West.

Now, of course, the original diagnosis was probably incorrect. And since I certainly did not know what I was doing, I can hardly attribute this outcome, one of the best that I have had in a long career, to anything that I may have said or done. But wait! I did do one or two things that might have been useful to Mrs. Brown. For one thing, I never completely gave up hope that things might change for her and that something good could come from our meetings. And also, whatever else I thought I was doing—and at that point my head was stuffed full of theories about psychoanalytic technique—I was somehow able to allow the hate and the love that naturally emerge in the psychoanalytic situation to surface in me without too much denial or repression and just allow them to do their own work.

What do I mean by hate and love that naturally emerge in the psychoanalytic situation? Let me focus on love, since that is what I am discussing, although I do believe that love and hate have an intimate and codependent relationship and that most human beings need easy access to both their love and their hate in order to maintain their narcissistic balance and mental health. For, even if the analyst cannot learn to understand and love the patient's hate for him, he must at least learn to respect it. And I think we must assume that, even during periods of the most intense rage and destructiveness, the patient might usually prefer to love us and be loved by us if only he knew how to manage it.

But picture to yourself two people—who know nothing about each other and have never met before—being brought into a room and asked to look into each other's eyes for as long as possible. Many years ago I tried this at the first meeting of a psychology seminar, and it aroused such powerful emotions in some students that I have never tried it again. One student seemed convinced that, as if by voodoo magic, she would have to fall in love with whomever she was gazing at, a thought akin to the fear of some that going into analysis means falling in love with their analyst.

And yet that is not so strange a fantasy after all. Over the last few decades an immense amount of research has been done on the mutual gazing activities of mother and infant, research that involves filming both mother and child and frame-by-frame analysis of the exquisitely delicate interactions that constitute this apparently simple activity. We have learned that the normal infant is eager to gaze, and that there is something very wrong if a child refuses to look. Yet as avid as the child is to gaze, there is a natural rhythm to this activity and at some point the child becomes overly excited and tries to avert his gaze in order to calm himself down. Those mothers who do not permit their child to look away and so regulate their own excitement may become involved in an interaction that Beebe and Stern (1977) have called "chase and dodge," in which the mother pursues the child with her gaze while he tries to avoid looking at her and ends up frustrated or crying. Consequently, an originally loving interaction may over time become converted into a perverse activity that ends in pain and anger rather than pleasure and love.

But if the mother is sensitive to the baby's internal rhythms and if many other things go well enough, then the baby normally falls in love with his mother just as the mother will normally fall in love with her baby. Since this mutual love occurs in the natural order of things, it may not, after all, be so surprising that some people are still afraid that if they gaze long enough at a stranger who enthusiastically returns their gaze they might become overwhelmed and unable to extricate themselves from an attachment they might otherwise not desire.

In fact, paying very close attention in a particular kind of way has at many times and in many cultures been considered a method of aspiring to a special relationship with oneself, with one's neighbors, or with God. Eastern meditation practice and yoga teach us to pay close attention to our breathing or to the utterance of a single syllable or mantra, while mystics and academics alike may devote their entire lives to the close study of a single text or even a single poem. Such close attention, unswervingly maintained over a long period of time, may come to resemble what we know as prayer, and, if I recall correctly, the French mystic Simone Weil (1950) once maintained that any activity a person may choose, shoe repair, for example, if carried out with a certain quality of attention and sufficient devotion, does indeed become the moral equivalent of prayer.

Psychoanalysts are not engaged in anything so practical as shoe repair. But what might it be like if a psychoanalyst were to try to pay the same kind of close attention to a patient, the kind of attention that might indeed be the moral equivalent of prayer? As I try to imagine this situation, it seems that, first of all, you would have to be thinking about the patient quite a lot, not only during his sessions but also at other times throughout the day so that, in an ongoing way, he would become a constantly living presence in your memory and in your life. Let's call this "living presence." Second, if you were voluntarily going to be living with the patient in your mind so much of the time, it seems to me that you would have to trust that he was basically a good person. Let's call this "basic trust." Third, no matter what his problems or how upset, angry, or unpleasant he might be at any particular moment, you would have to feel that underneath it all the patient is a person for whom you have some real sympathy and with whom you might be able to do some useful work. Let's call this "sympathetic resonance."

If you can find this basic trust in the patient, feel sympathetic resonance with him, and hold him in your mind so that he becomes a living presence, then you have become connected to him in a very special way. In my experience, the effects of this kind of attention and connection maintained over a long period of time can be very profound indeed, for the person with whom you are thus connected, whether patient or friend or lover, begins to feel held together by your attention and to feel that more and more parts of himself are becoming meaningfully interconnected.

People who know us only in passing know only a small portion of us, some particular aspect, perhaps only that part we wish to show to them or to the world. The better people get to know us, the more and more parts of us they get to know. And, if someone can accept and embrace parts of us that may be disconnected and that even we do not want to know about, then that attention can heal us and help us feel more whole.

You may have noticed that I have just given you my personal prescription for love but, unlike a prescription for Prozac or Paxil, it unfortunately cannot be filled at the nearest drugstore. The advantage it has, though, is that you do not need a diploma, a state license, or even a couch to prescribe it. It can be used by anyone, anywhere, at any time—without any ritual or hocus-pocus. But it is definitely not an easy task. Shamans, mystics, saints and other very special people know how to do this, and some have attained this ability only after years of seeking and struggle while others seem just naturally gifted.

For those patients for whom I am able to provide something even vaguely approaching this kind of attention while still maintaining my own narcissistic balance—and I do not always try to do this, and even when I try I am often not successful—the most curious things begin to happen. After a while you find yourself totally emotionally involved in the process and you are no longer doing it because you are a doctor or a paid professional but, rather, because you are caught up in a process that is larger than yourself. A part of you is still able to observe professionally, to reflect and exercise control, but another part is hopelessly entangled, and you simply cannot help it. You have, to speak quite frankly, fallen in love with your patient.

If I had an attorney, he would at this point caution me to strike the last sentence. He would point out that it will not only lose me referrals but that it may very likely invalidate my malpractice insurance. I can well understand why Freud spoke only in private, to his most trusted colleagues, about the role of love in the therapeutic process. One hundred years later, very little has really changed. Any HMO will still pay thousands of dollars for elaborate magnetic resonance imaging of chronic back pain but not a penny for therapeutic touch. Both the American Psychiatric and the American Psychological Associations have drawn up elaborate protocols for the best evidence-based treatments for specific mental disorders, including cognitive therapy for depression and powerful psychoactive drugs for this and other conditions. No one mentions love, although there is probably as large a body of research on the positive effects of care, attention, and love on the body and mind as there is on the effects of most of these other reimbursable therapeutic modalities.

For example, research in cognitive neurobiology (Schore, 1994; Hofer, 2003) has made it abundantly clear that the mother's language and emotional reactions psychobiologically influence the production of hormones and neurotransmitters in the child's brain, so that the emotional interactions between mother and infant are configured into the developing nervous system. In this way, the mother's mind directly alters the child's body and nervous system. It would seem that a sane society should honor and support its mothers as well as its psychopharmacologists and brain surgeons, for the good-enough mother is subtly creating what the brain specialist can only grossly attempt to repair. Furthermore, I believe that psychoanalysts and therapists need to be constantly aware that their own words and actions also influence the production of hormones and neurotransmitters in the patient's brain in ways similar to the psychoactive drugs, but sometimes with greater precision and fewer side effects. So the power of paying a certain kind of attention or of loving another human being can be very great indeed.

I mentioned earlier some people's concerns that, if they went into analysis, they would inevitably fall in love with their analyst, and I also maintained that not everyone who goes into psychoanalysis falls in love with their analyst. But, in my view, if, after some long period of particularly close attention, patients do in fact fall in love with their psychoanalyst, then they are very lucky indeed. For if they have truly fallen in love with their analyst, then their analyst is very likely to have fallen in love with them, and when this happens, then the *world becomes enchanted again,* just as it was in days of happy childhood or as we sometimes find it in fairy tales.

Some of you may remember that wonderful scene in Tolstoy's (1877) *Anna Karenina* when Levin first discovers that Kitty, who previously rejected him, now loves him. Levin writes down only the first letter of each word of a long, complicated sentence, but Kitty immediately deciphers his meaning and responds with an initialed sentence of her own, whose meaning, in turn, he immediately comprehends. Their minds are in that state of perfect sympathetic resonance so characteristic of love, and Levin, neither eating nor sleeping, spends all that night and the next morning in a trance. When he walks through the streets to her house to speak with her parents, the world seems magically enchanted. He watches the children going to school, the pigeons on the street, the rolls in a bakery window covered with flour, and everything he sees takes on a significance of unearthly beings which makes him laugh and cry for joy (pp. 397, 403).

Anyone who is lucky enough to have known the magic of love will recognize this enchantment of the world and understand why people will risk their lives to attain it. It is also understandable why less fortunate people will spend their days in altered states of consciousness—like being high on drugs—to mimic or parody this state. Of course, unlike fairy tales, this reenchantment of the world may not last forever, but as long as it does last it is marvelous and astonishing, and it revitalizes the world in a way that amplifies its meaning and makes it seem wonderfully worthwhile to be alive. And even when disenchantment takes place, if it occurs relatively slowly and painlessly, as it sometimes does in real life when the bloom of love becomes tarnished by the corrosive action of reality and only the memory of love remains, then people may still feel that something wonderful once happened to them.

Freud maintained that the finding of a beloved person is always a refinding, that we are always seeking to find once again the people we loved in our earliest life. Homer also knew that recognition is the pathway to love, and one of the most touching scenes in all literature takes place when Penelope hesitates to recognize Odysseus, who has come back to her as an unknown stranger after 20 years of wandering.

For seeing comes before words, and perhaps the immediate power of recognition comes from the primordial reciprocity found in mother–infant gazing. But there is another kind of recognition that is also important. I will illustrate with a story I have always enjoyed. There used to be a popular cocktail called a Grasshopper. Well, one day an actual grasshopper walked into the bar at the Ritz and sat down, waiting to be served. The bartender approached him with a smile and said, "We're very pleased to have you here! You know, we have a cocktail named after you." And the grasshopper, equally pleased, replied, "Really, you do? You have a cocktail named Irving?"

From this story we learn that the most important thing to Irving, as well as to the rest of us, is not to be recognized generically as a grasshopper, but to be known in our absolute individual uniqueness as Irving. When we are not recognized or when we are misrecognized, we experience shame and humiliation, but when we are fully recognized in our uniqueness, we experience gratitude and love. This recognition that we seek is complex, for it includes both the feeling that we belong to a category larger than ourselves such as grasshoppers or human beings, as well as the sense that within that belonging we are absolutely special, as we know ourselves to be.

In the early months mother and baby feel at one with each other, for they are in love. We think that it takes a baby about a year and a half to recognize fully its physical separateness from its mother, and perhaps another three or four years to recognize fully its psychic separateness. In those few years the baby has made an extraordinary voyage, from merger and absolute dependence to separateness and interdependence, but it would be a voyage that might end in isolation were it not for our need to refind love.

I believe that when we look for love we search for recognition, for a sign that some person whose uniqueness of body and mind we have glimpsed has also caught sight of our own uniqueness of body and mind and delights in it. When this mutual recognition clicks in, we experience the exhilaration and sense of fulfillment of feeling, even for a moment, that someone truly knows us and that we truly know him. When we have loving sex we feel physically known in that way, and when we have moments of intimacy we feel spiritually known in that way. It is the cumulation of such moments of mutual recognition that makes for good parenting, good friendships, good marriages, and even, in my opinion, good psychoanalysis.

REFERENCES

Ainsworth, M. D. S., Blehar, M. C., Waters, E. & Wall, S. (1978), *Patterns of Attachment: A Psychological Study of the Strange Situation*. Mahwah, NJ: Lawrence Erlbaum Associates.

Akhtar, S. & Thomson, J. A. (1982), Overview: Narcissistic personality disorder. *Amer. J. Psychiat.*, 139:12–20.

Aron, L. (1995), The internalized primal scene. *Psychoanal. Dial.*, 5:195–237.

_____ (2000), Self-reflexivity and the therapeutic action of psychoanalysis. *Psychoanal. Psychol.*, 17:667–689.

_____ (2001), *A Meeting of Minds: Mutuality in Psychoanalysis*. Hillsdale, NJ: The Analytic Press.

Auerbach, J. S. (1990), Narcissism: Reflections on others' images of an elusive concept. *Psychoanal. Psychol.*, 7:545–564.

_____ (1993), The origins of narcissism and narcissistic personality disorder: A theoretical and empirical reformulation. In: *Empirical Studies of Psychoanalytic Theories, Vol. 4: Psychoanalytic Perspectives on Psychopathology*, ed. J. M. Masling & R. F. Bornsteen. Washington, DC: American Psychological Association, pp. 43–110.

Bach, S. (1977), On the narcissistic state of consciousness. *Internat. J. Psycho-Anal.*, 58:209–233.

———— (1985), *Narcissistic States and the Therapeutic Process*. Northvale, NJ: Aronson.

———— (1991), On sadomasochistic object relations. In: *Perversions and Near-Perversions in Clinical Practice: New Psychoanalytic Perspectives*, ed. G. Fogel & W. Myers. New Haven, CT: Yale University Press, pp. 75–92.

———— (1994), *The Language of Perversion and the Language of Love*. Northvale, NJ: Aronson.

———— & Schwartz, L. (1972), A dream of the Marquis de Sade. *J. Amer. Psychoanal. Assn.*, 20:451–475.

Balint, M. (1960), Primary narcissism and primary love. *Psychoanal. Quart.*, 29:6–43.

———— (1968), *The Basic Fault: Therapeutic Aspects of Regression*. London: Tavistock.

Beckett, S. (1957), *Proust*. New York: Grove Press.

Beebe, B. & Lachmann, F. (2005), *Infant Research and Adult Treatment: Co-constructing Interactions*. Hillsdale, NJ: The Analytic Press.

———— & Stern, D. (1977), Engagement–disengagement and early object experiences. In: *Communicative Structures and Psychic Structures*, ed. N. Freedman & S. Grand. New York: Plenum Press, pp. 35–55.

Benjamin, J. (1988), *The Bonds of Love: Psychoanalysis, Feminism, and the Problem of Domination*. New York: Pantheon.

———— (2004), Beyond doer and done to: An intersubjective view of thirdness. *Psychoanal. Quart.*, 73:5–46.

Bergman, P. & Escalona, S. (1949), Unusual sensitivities in very young children. *The Psychoanalytic Study of the Child*, 4:333–352. New York: International Universities Press.

Bohr, N. (1963), *Essays 1958–1962 on Atomic Physics and Human Knowledge*. New York: Interscience.

Borges, J. L. (1962), Funes, the memorius. In: *Ficciones*, ed. A. Kerrigan. New York: Grove Press, pp. 107–115.

Brabant, E., Falzeder, E. & Giampieri-Deutsch, P., eds. (1993), *The Correspondence of Sigmund Freud and Sándor Ferenczi, Vol. 1, 1908–1914*. Cambridge, MA: Belknap Press.

Bruner, J. (1968), *Processes of Cognitive Growth: Infancy*. Worcester, MA: Clark University Press.

Busch, F. (2005), Conflict theory/trauma theory. *Psychoanal. Quart.*, 74:27–45.

Castle, T. (1995), *The Female Thermometer: Eighteenth-Century Culture and the Invention of the Uncanny*. New York: Oxford University Press.

Coates, S. (1998), Having a mind of one's own and holding the other in mind: Commentary on paper by Peter Fonagy and Mary Target. *Psychoanal. Dial.*, 8:115–148.

Eagle, M. N. (1984), *Recent Developments in Psychoanalysis: A Critical Evaluation.* New York: McGraw-Hill.

Ellman, S. (1998), Enactment, transference, and analytic trust. In: *Enactment*, ed. S. Ellman & M. Moskowitz. Northvale, NJ: Aronson, pp. 183–204.

———— (in press), *Psychoanalytic Theory: A Contemporary Integration.*

———— & Carsky, M. (2002), Symbolization and the development of interpretable transference. In: *Symbolization and Desymbolization: Essays in Honor of Norbert Freedman*, ed. R. Lasky. London: Karnac Books, pp. 280–305.

Erikson, E. (1956), The problem of ego identity. *J. Amer. Psychoanal. Assn.*, 4:56–121.

Ferenczi, S. (1932), *The Clinical Diary of Sándor Ferenczi*, ed. J. Dupont (trans. M. Balint & N. Z. Jackson). Cambridge, MA: Harvard University Press, 1988.

———— (1933), Confusion of tongues between adults and children. In: *Final Contributions to the Problems and Methods of Psycho-Analysis.* London: Hogarth Press, 1955, pp. 156–167.

Fitzgerald, F. S. (1945), *The Crack-Up*, ed. E. Wilson. New York: New Directions.

Fonagy, P. (1999), Memory and therapeutic action. *Internat. J. Psycho-Anal.*, 80:215–223.

———— Gurgely, G., Jurist, E. & Target, M. (2002), *Affect Regulation, Mentalization, and the Development of the Self.* New York: Other Press.

———— Steele, M., Steele, H., Moran, G. & Higgitt, A. (1991), The capacity for understanding mental states: The reflective self in parent and child and its significance for security of attachment. *Infant Ment. Health J.*, 12:201–217.

Freedman, N. & Berzofsky, M. (1995), Shape of the communicated transference in difficult and not-so-difficult patients: Symbolized and de-symbolized transference. *Psychoanal. Psychol.*, 12:363–374.

———— Hoffenberg, J. D., Vorus, N. & Frosch, A. (1999), The effectiveness of psychoanalytic psychotherapy. *J. Amer. Psychoanal. Assn.*, 47:741–772.

Freud, A. (1967), About losing and being lost. *The Psychoanalytic Study of the Child*, 22:16–23. New York: International Universities Press.

Freud, S. (1896), Further remarks on the neuro-psychoses of defense. *Standard Edition*, 3:159–185. London: Hogarth Press, 1962.

———— (1914), Remembering, repeating and working-through: Further recommendations on the technique of psychoanalysis II. *Standard Edition*, 12:145–156. London: Hogarth Press, 1958.

_____ (1915a), Observations on transference love. *Standard Edition,* 12:159–171. London: Hogarth Press, 1958.

_____ (1915b), The unconscious. *Standard Edition,* 14:161–215. London: Hogarth Press, 1957.

_____ (1919), A child is being beaten: A contribution to the study of the origin of sexual perversions. *Standard Edition,* 17:175–204. London: Hogarth Press, 1955.

_____ (1924), The loss of reality in neurosis and psychosis. *Standard Edition,* 19:181–187. London: Hogarth Press, 1966.

_____ (1930), Civilization and its discontents. *Standard Edition,* 21: 64–145. London: Hogarth Press, 1961.

Furman, R. & Furman, E. (1984), Intermittent de-cathexis—A type of parental dysfunction. *Internat. J. Psycho-Anal.,* 65:423–434.

Gedo, J. (1984), *Psychoanalysis and Its Discontents.* New York: Guilford Press.

George, C., Kaplan, N. & Main, M. (1984, 1985, 1996), Adult Attachment Interview. Unpublished protocol, 3rd ed., Department of Psychology, University of California, Berkeley.

Grotjahn, M. (1967), Sigmund Freud and the art of letter writing. In: *Freud as We Knew Him,* ed. H. M. Ruitenbeek. Detroit, MI: Wayne State University Press, 1973, pp. 433–447.

Grunes, M. (1984), The therapeutic object relationship. *Psychoanal. Rev.,* 71:123–143.

_____ (1998), The therapeutic object relationship—2. In: *The Modern Freudians: Contemporary Psychoanalytic Technique,* ed. C. S. Ellman, S. Grand, M. Silvan & S. Ellman. Northvale, NJ: Aronson, pp. 129–140.

Haynal, A. (1988), *Controversies in Psychoanalytic Method: From Freud and Ferenczi to Michael Balint.* New York: New York University Press.

Hofer, M. (2003), The emerging neurobiology of attachment and separation: How parents shape their infant's brain and behavior. In: *September 11: Trauma and Human Bonds,* ed. S. Coates, J. Rosenthal & D. Schechter. Hillsdale, NJ: The Analytic Press, pp. 191–209.

Homer (800 BCE), *The Odyssey,* trans. S. Butler. New York: Barnes & Noble Book, 1999.

Kermode, F. (1999), *Not Entitled.* New York: Farrar, Straus & Giroux.

Klein, M. (1946), Notes on some schizoid mechanisms. *Internat. J. Psycho-Anal.,* 27:99–110.

Kohut, H. (1959), Introspection, empathy, and psychoanalysis—An examination of the relationship between mode of observation and theory. *J. Amer. Psychoanal. Assn.,* 7:459–483.

_____ (1966), Forms and transformations of narcissism. *J. Amer. Psychoanal. Assn.,* 14:243–272.

_____ (1971), *The Analysis of the Self.* New York: International Universities Press.

_____ (1977), *The Restoration of the Self*. New York: International Universities Press.

Kris, A. (1984), The conflicts of ambivalence. *The Psychoanalytic Study of the Child*, 39:213–234. New Haven, CT: Yale University Press.

_____ (1985), Resistance in divergent and convergent conflicts. *Psychoanal. Quart.*, 54:537–568.

Loewald, H. (1980), The waning of the Oedipus complex. In: *Papers on Psychoanalysis*. New Haven, CT: Yale University Press, pp. 384–404.

_____ (1981), Regression: Some general considerations. *Psychoanal. Quart.*, 50:22–43.

Mahler, M. (1963), Thoughts about development and individuation. *The Psychoanalytic Study of the Child*, 18:307–324. New York: International Universities Press.

Main, M. (2000), The organized categories of infant, child and adult attachment : Flexible vs. inflexible attention under attachment-related stress. *J. Amer. Psychoanalytic Assn.*, 48:1055–1096.

_____ & Hesse, E. (1992), Disorganized/disoriented infant behavior in the Strange Situation, lapses in the monitoring of reasoning and discourse during the parent's Adult Attachment Interview, and dissociative states. In: *Attachment and Psychoanalysis*, ed. M. Ammaniti & D. Stern. Rome: Gius, Laterza & Figli, pp. 86–140.

McGuire, W. (1974), *The Freud/Jung Letters: The Correspondence Between Sigmund Freud and C. G. Jung*, ed. W. McGuire (trans. R. Mannheim & R. F. C. Hull). Princeton, NJ: Princeton University Press.

Milosz, C. (1986), *Unattainable Earth*, trans. C. Milosz & R. Hass. Hopewell, NJ: Ecco Press.

Modell, A. H. (1990), *Other Times, Other Realities*. Cambridge, MA: Harvard University Press.

Molière, R. W. (1670), *The Bourgeois Gentleman*. Dover, 2001.

Nader, K., Schafe, G. & LeDoux, J. (2000), Fear memories require protein synthesis in the amygdala for reconsolidation after retrieval. *Nature*, 406:722–726.

New York Times, April 30, 1996, Section A, p. 4.

Nunberg, H. & Federn, E., eds. (1962), *Minutes of the Vienna Psychoanalytic Society, Vol. 1: 1906–1908*. New York: International Universities Press.

Ogden, T. H. (1985), On potential space. *Internat. J. Psycho-Anal.*, 66:129–141.

Orlinsky, D. E. & Geller, J. D. (1993). Patients' representations of therapy: A new focus of psychotherapy research. In: *Psychodynamic Research: A Handbook for Clinical Practice*, ed. N. Miller, L. Luborsky, J. B. Barber & J. P. Docherty. New York: Basic Books, pp. 423–460.

Proust, M. (1913–1927), *Remembrance of Things Past*, trans. C. K. Scott Moncrieff & T. Kilmartin. New York: Knopf, 1982.

Rapaport, D. (1951), *Organization and Pathology of Thought: Selected Sources*. New York: Columbia University Press.

_____ Gill, M. & Schafer, R. (1945), *Diagnostic Psychological Testing, Vol. 1*. Chicago: Year Book Publishers.

_____ _____ & _____ (1946), *Diagnostic Psychological Testing, Vol. 2*. Chicago: Year Book Publishers.

Schore, A. N. (1994), *Affect Regulation and the Origin of the Self: The Neurobiology of Emotional Development*. Hillsdale, NJ: Lawrence Erlbaum Associates.

Slade, A. (2004), The move from categories to process: Attachment phenomena and clinical evaluation. *Infant Ment. Health J.*, 25:269–283.

Spitz, R. (1945), Hospitalism: An inquiry into the genesis of psychiatric conditions in early childhood. *The Psychoanalytic Study of the Child*, 1:53–74. New York: International Universities Press.

_____ (1965), *The First Year of Life*. New York: International Universities Press.

Steingart, I. (1995), *A Thing Apart: Love and Reality in the Therapeutic Relationship*. Northvale, NJ: Aronson.

Stern, D. (1998), The process of therapeutic change involving implicit knowledge: Some implications of developmental observations for adult psychotherapy. *Infant Ment. Health J.*, 19:300–308.

Teicher, M., Polcari, A., Anderson, S., Anderson, C. & Navalta, C. (2003), Neurobiological effects of childhood stress and trauma. In: *September 11: Trauma and Human Bonds*, ed. S. Coates, J. Rosenthal & D. Schechter. Hillsdale, NJ: The Analytic Press.

Tolstoy, L. (1869), *War and Peace*, trans. C. Garnett. New York: Random House, 2002.

_____ (1887), *Anna Karenina*, trans. R. Pevear & L. Volokhonsky. New York: Penguin Books, 2004.

Tronick, E. (1998), Dyadically expanded states of consciousness and the process of therapeutic change. *Infant Ment. Health J.*, 19:290–299.

_____ Als, H., Adamson, L., Wise, S. & Brazelton, T. (1978), The infant's response to entrapment between contradictory messages in face-to-face interaction. *J. Amer. Acad. Child & Adolesc. Psychiat.*, 17:1–13.

Vygotsky, L. S. (1978), *Mind in Society: The Development of Higher Psychological Processes*, ed. M. Cole, V. John-Steiner, S. Scribner & E. Suberman. Cambridge, MA: Harvard University Press.

Weil, S. (1950), *Attente de Dieu*. Paris: Fayard, 1985.

Winnicott, D. W. (1945), Primitive emotional development. *Internat. J. Psycho-Anal.*, 26:137–143.

_____ (1953), Transitional objects and transitional phenomena—A study of the first not-me possession. *Internat. J. Psycho-Anal.*, 34:89–97.

_____ (1955), Metapsychological and clinical aspects of regression within the psycho-analytical set-up. *Internat. J. Psycho-Anal.*, 36:16–26.

_____ (1956), Primary maternal preoccupation. In: *Collected Papers: Through Paediatrics to Psycho-Analysis*. New York: Basic Books.

_____ (1965), *The Maturational Processes and the Facilitating Environment*. New York: International Universities Press.

_____ (1967), Mirror-role of mother and family in child development. In: *Playing and Reality*. New York: Basic Books, pp. 111–118.

_____ (1971), *Playing and Reality*. New York: Basic Books.

Young-Bruehl, E. (1988), *Anna Freud: A Biography*. New York: Summit Books.

INDEX

About the Author

Sheldon Bach, Ph.D. is a Fellow of the Institute for Psychoanalytic Training and Research and of the International Psychoanalytical Association. Dr. Bach is Adjunct Clinical Professor of Psychology at the New York University Postdoctoral Program in Psychotherapy and Psychoanalysis and a faculty member and training analyst at the New York Freudian Society. The author of *Narcissistic States and the Therapeutic Process* (1985) and *The Language of Perversion and the Language of Love* (1994), he is in private practice in New York City.